THE SEAL OF
CAROLYN WARRENDER
SUCCESSFUL STENCILLING

CAROLYN WARRENDER'S BOOK OF STENCILLING

Carolyn Warrender

Tessa Strickland

HARMONY BOOKS

NEW YORK

Published in the United States of America in 1989 by Harmony Books, a division of Crown Publishers, Inc., 225 Park Avenue South, New York, New York 10003.

Published in Great Britain in 1988 by André Deutsch Limited, 105 106 Great Russell Street, London WC1B 3LJ, England.

HARMONY and colophon are trademarks of Crown Publishers

Manufactured in Italy.

Library of Congress Cataloging-in-Publication Data
Warrender, Carolyn.
[Book of Stencilling]
Carolyn Warrender's book of stencilling/Carolyn Warrender, Tessa Strickland.
    p.   cm.
Bibliography: p.
Includes index.
1. Stencil work.   I. Strickland, Tessa.   II. Title.   III. Title.
Book of Stencilling.
TT270.W37   1988
745.7′3 dc19   88–28677

ISBN 0–517–57238–9

10 9 8 7 6 5 4 3 2 1

First American Edition

For Francis and Robert

CONTENTS

FOREWORD

I HAVE been interested in interior design for as long as I can remember, and fascinated by the way in which people live in, and decorate, their homes.

During my professional life, I have been lucky enough to work for some of the most innovative and successful design groups in the world. Each in its own way has played a different part in moulding what I had absorbed in earlier years into the style that I now have the opportunity to project through Carolyn Warrender, Stencil Designs Ltd.

At Colefax and Fowler, my first real job, I received the best possible training in the interior design principles established by John Fowler and continued by Tom Parr. Later, I was able to share the wonderful insight and talent of Bernard and the late Laura Ashley, during the three fascinating years I spent with them researching and developing the home furnishings side of their business.

As I gained more experience in my chosen profession, I became aware of the enormous possibilities that existed for co-ordination in the home. At the same time, I also felt that these possibilities could only be realised by those who could afford to employ a professional designer, or who had a strong artistic sense themselves. Without these advantages, it was difficult for thousands of home owners to give decoration that extra stamp of flair and originality, in spite of the fact that more and more ranges of home furnishings were being launched every season.

What, then, was the missing ingredient? A trip to America in the early eighties gave me the answer – and it lay in the decoration of a house that had once belonged to an early pilgrim settler. Everywhere I looked, walls, floors, fabrics and furniture had been stencilled in beautiful, complementary patterns. I

realised instantly that this was what I had been seeking. I had always enjoyed stencilling as a child; now I saw that this technique could give a new dimension to contemporary home decoration, and create many more opportunities for self-expression and original design among the growing numbers of people who wanted to decorate their homes themselves. What was more, the pre-cut stencilling kits produced by companies such as Adele Bishop and Stencil-Ease, whose ranges I now sell, made stencilling an extremely economical way of achieving co-ordination in the home.

My enthusiasm led me to open the first specialist stencil store in central London in 1984. Last year saw the company move to larger premises in Lower Sloane Street, SW1, where visitors can browse through an enormous range of stencils and stencilling equipment, and try stencilling for themselves with no obligation

under the supervision of our trained staff. I also hold regular stencilling workshops, and I have yet to find anyone who at the end of the day is not producing beautiful results. Even the most nervous beginners are astonished by the speed and ease with which they can master stencilling techniques.

I have had great fun creating this book, and I must give special thanks to Tessa Strickland for a very happy and stimulating working partnership. On the following pages, we have tried to show as great a variety as possible of stencilling styles, reflecting both my own work and that of many others, including amateurs, in order to show the endless possibilities that exist within the world of stencilling. Who knows? Perhaps for you, as it was for me, stencilling will be the start of an adventure that will inspire you to change the way you decorate your home forever.

Carolyn Warrender.

— 9 —

INTRODUCTION

Even if you think you are new to stencilling, you have probably stencilled before. Stop for a moment and cast your mind back to your early schooldays. Do you remember sitting at your desk and doodling with those sheets of plastic that had squares and triangles and other odd shapes punched out of them? Do you remember cutting your own designs from cardboard during art classes at a time when it didn't matter too much if you painted your face and your hands as well as the paper in front of you? This is stencilling at its simplest — and you need little more skill than you had as a child to take up stencilling again and use it for home decoration. For, unlike most art forms, stencilling does not require long hours of practice. Anyone can do it.

What, then, is a stencil and what is the secret of successful stencilling? A stencil is a thin sheet of durable and flexible material out of which a pattern has been cut. When the stencil is laid on the surface which is to be decorated and paint is applied over the stencil, the paint can extend only as far as the borders of the chosen pattern since the stencil acts as a shield and protects the background surface from being painted other than in those precise areas defined by the pattern. To stencil successfully, you need to ensure that this background surface is suitable for stencil paints, to measure and plan your design before you start, to apply the stencil paint lightly and to select colours and designs that are appropriate to the room or object you want to decorate.

As a method of combining colours and patterns to create a decorative scheme, you will find that stencilling has many obvious advantages:

First, it is versatile. In any room, you can choose the surfaces on which you wish to stencil. You can control the colour of these background surfaces, and the colour of the stencils themselves. You are entirely free to be as discreet or flamboyant as you like in the positioning of your stencils. You are free, too, to use the stencils on their own or to combine them with wallpapers or with a number of different paint finishes.

Secondly, stencilling will enable you to create and reproduce the design of your choice more quickly and effectively than by any other means. It is certainly quicker than drawing freehand or tracing an outline and then colouring it in. It also guarantees an accurate and consistent result.

Thirdly, stencils are economical both in terms of your money and your time.

Nineteenth-century wall stencilling at the Church of St Swithun, Compton Beauchamp

After your initial investment in brushes, paints and stencil kits you will find pre-cut stencils are virtually indestructible, provided they are properly looked after, and can be used again and again. You may need to give yourself a reasonable amount of time to tackle your first project, but you will find that the technicalities of stencilling are easily mastered and once you have practised once or twice you will be surprised by how quickly you will be able to work.

Above all, stencilling will give you the freedom to create decorative schemes which, simply because they are the result of your own imagination and creativity, will have an individuality that cannot be matched by any mass-produced paper or fabric designs. As your stencilling progresses you will probably be tempted to combine different stencils in the same room, but even if you were to tackle a room with one stencil and one pot of paint, you would be able to interpret the spaces and the surfaces around you in a huge variety of ways. You could also take the same stencil and use it in different ways and with different colours in other parts of your house. For while stencilling is simple to master, it is infinite in its uses and effects.

The History of Stencils

Because it is such an easy yet effective way of creating shapes and patterns, people have practised the art of stencilling for thousands of years. The earliest evidence is fragmentary and we can only guess at its origins, but there are numerous examples of primitive stencilled designs on fabric, pottery and a variety of other artefacts made in China, Indonesia and South East Asia, as well as the Near East. It is likely that stencilling was used as a decorative form by the ancient Egyptians as early as 2500BC. These designs from one of the greatest early civilizations still have a wonderful appeal today, and Egyptian motifs are a delight for contemporary stencil artists. Bored by brushing your teeth at a plain white basin in a plain white bathroom? You won't be if you make it Egyptian.

In ancient China, stencilling was first confined to religious subjects, and the earliest examples we know of can be seen in Western China, at the Caves of the Thousand Buddhas, in Tunhuang. But, gradually, secular as well as religious artists turned to stencilling as a medium and intricate designs were used to decorate silk cloth and garments. The silk trade would take the skill to other countries of the Far East as well as to India and Persia. In Japan, the art form reached new heights with the discovery of a method for waterproofing mulberry fibres by using the juices of the persimmon. The dried mulberry sheets could be cut with great precision, and a wealth of elaborate designs was created, with artists taking their inspiration from the country's flora and fauna and the rich, subtle and ever-changing colours of the Japanese seasons. Let your thoughts and designs be inspired in turn by the colours and patterns you see around you in the natural world of today.

The trade route that flourished between East and West slowly brought stencilling across to Europe, where it enjoyed widespread popularity as a form of decoration in the medieval period. Before the advent of printing, stencils were used to illustrate books and playing cards. Stencilling was also extensively used in painting architectural ornament on the walls of churches throughout the Gothic and Renaissance periods, and in the houses of the wealthy it soon had a place alongside mural painting as a form of interior decoration. In the right environment, stencils enjoy a long life and some lovely examples of stencilled interiors can still be seen in northern churches and castles, and in the old villas and palaces of southern Europe.

TOP LEFT: *A fragment of early eighteenth-century ceiling paper, printed with woodblocks and coloured with stencils.*
BOTTOM LEFT: *Kozo paper stencil, stained and toughened with persimmon juice (Japan, early nineteenth century).*
FAR RIGHT: *Stencilled wall decorations from 'Joscelyns', Little Horkesley, Essex.*

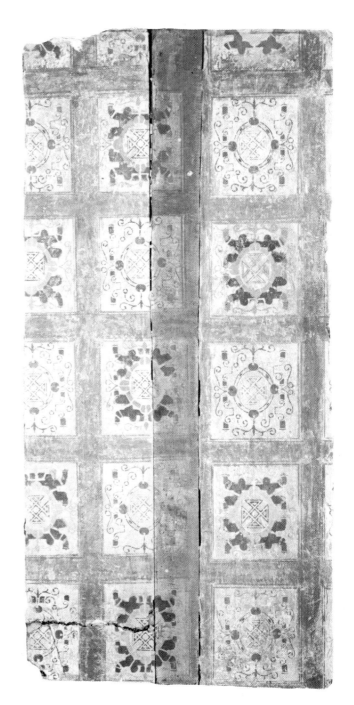

The introduction of wallpaper to Europe in the late seventeenth century presented new opportunities for stencillers and one of the most dramatic uses of stencils over the last three hundred years has been in the manufacture of flock wallpapers, produced by painting size

Early seventeenth-century flock on canvas design. The flock was applied using stencil templates.

over a stencil to form a sticky 'brocade' pattern, to which small tufts of silk or cotton were made to adhere. Fragments remain of a number of seventeenth- and eighteenth-century wallpapers, where stencilling has been chosen as an alternative to printing, and contemporary sources suggest that this form of decoration came to be considered appropriate in the reception rooms of the burgeoning middle classes in England and also in the lesser rooms of grand houses. Meanwhile, for that sector of the population which could not afford wallpaper, stencilling direct onto furniture, floors or wall surfaces was a cheap and effective way of brightening their surroundings.

But it was in nineteenth-century America that stencilling really flowered as a decorative art form for simple domestic households. With limited building materials and limited funds, the early settlers soon discovered that they could transform their makeshift surroundings into colourful and attractive homes by using stencils. Unable to afford or obtain the rich fabrics and wallpapers that were fashionable in Europe at the time, they could nevertheless imitate the designs by cutting patterns onto stencils and repeating them on their walls. Individual householders often made and applied their own designs, but itinerant craftsmen also travelled from village to village with their paints, brushes and templates. Scenes and plants from the natural world

were also an inspiration both to householders and to professional artists, and the considerable charm of American stencils is due partly to the wonderful balance of the earth and vegetable pigments that were used and partly to the simple, arcadian and acadian designs.

Back in England, stencilling became a popular theme in Victorian decoration, and the later Art Deco and Art Nouveau styles also drew on this art form. But, since the beginning of this century, the mass production of wallpaper had for many years eclipsed the older art of stencilling. Then, in the 1960s, Adele Bishop started a stencilling business in the USA that was to expand by leaps and bounds, inspiring many amateur artists as well as professional designers and making the art form as popular as it had been in the early pioneering days.

Many companies in Europe and North America now produce a wide range of pre-cut stencils that put this art form within the reach of people everywhere. At a time when many of us live in houses that are uniform in design and appearance, when space is at a premium and function often takes priority over individuality, stencilling provides the opportunity to create unique interiors that can be as sophisticated or simple, as co-ordinated or full of contrast as their owner wishes. Because it is unique in offering this kind of freedom, stencilling is here to stay.

These Shelburne stencils by Adele Bishop are inspired by the stencils at a house near Utica, New York, now on display at the Shelburne Museum, Vermont.

stencils — the patterns of shaded colour with their trim, clean edges sing out from any background surface with a clarity and freshness that delight even the most educated eye. Anyone who has been in a stencilled room will not be surprised to learn that the word derives from the Old French word *estenceler*, meaning 'to sparkle'. The kind of sparkle you want is entirely up to you. But whatever your taste — restrained elegance, bright primary colours, rustic simplicity — you can set about your work happy in the knowledge that the effect you achieve will be quite unique, and that you will have had the satisfaction of creating it yourself, exactly as you wanted it to be.

The following chapters have been written to help you discover just a few of the possibilities that stencilling has to offer. Please read them all — many of the ideas discussed in one chapter would be equally valid in another but they have not been repeated because of lack of space and for fear of having a monotonous text. Pay particular attention to the advice in Part I — as with any skill, you will derive the most enjoyment, and achieve the best results, if you take the trouble to learn the ground rules before you start. We hope that this book will open your eyes to many, many stencilling possibilities, and that reading this book will be the beginning of a long and happy love affair for you.

It is impossible to say that stencilling is not for you in any way. If you have not stencilled before, you will soon find that you become addicted. You may not be too confident about your artistic ability, but there is no need for you to start by tackling a complicated design. There is a curious charm about even the simplest

PART I

PRINCIPLES

ONE

STENCILLING PRINCIPLES

LOOKING FOR INSPIRATION

Whatever room you choose to stencil, think before you start. Sit in the room. Walk about in it. Lie on the floor and stare at the ceiling. What do you like about it? What do you dislike? Which features do you want to enhance, and which would be better concealed? Very few rooms are perfect in their proportions and characteristics, but with a little attention you should be able to turn any imperfections to your advantage. Let your imagination play games. If you live in a modern cube with no interesting features, think about stencilling in a dado rail, skirting board or *trompe l'oeil* panelling. If your bathroom has ugly Victorian pipes that you would prefer to have hidden, but you don't have the resources to change or conceal them, try stencilling tangled vines and creepers up and around the pipes and adding

a few real vines and rubber plants to create a jungle bathroom. Transform awkward beams and RSJs from eyesores into attractive features with your stencil kit.

Remember that a house is an adventure, both for you as its inhabitant and for your visitors. What will you find — what would you like to find — beyond the next door? One of the great delights about decorating, and in particular stencilling, your home is the chance you have to create different moods in different rooms, whilst uniting them all harmoniously in the house or apartment as a whole. The larger your home, the more scope you will have, but even a one-bedroom studio can offer enormous potential. Think, plan, experiment and you will be able to stencil your surroundings in such a way that they become lasting expressions of your own personality.

PROBLEM ROOMS

Different rooms present different problems. In some cases, the problem may not lie in the design of the room but in the taste of its previous occupant. It is difficult to gain a clear sense of a room's potential if the ceiling and walls have been painted in alternating zigzags of clashing colours. If the room you plan to decorate has been painted a colour you like and are happy to live with, well and good. If not, if it has furry wallpaper or an ill-advised paint scheme that you would rather live without, strip away the offending material as fast as possible.

Blue and white china from Deruta and Orvieto, Italy, was the inspiration behind this unusual border design, in which circular motifs are linked by the introduction of simple blue dots. The design is repeated on the cushions.

Don't shirk this stage — it's an exercise that can be more enjoyable than it may sound. Eliminating another's taste is a very gratifying exercise and you will probably be in excellent humour by the time you have finished. Next, make sure all of the surfaces you plan to decorate are well cleaned and sanded down, then paint on a white undercoat. You will find that you are looking at the room through new eyes. What do you see?

NO LIGHT

Dark rooms can to some extent be lightened by light, bright colours. But remember that if your room doesn't get any direct light, either because it faces north or because its light is blocked by a building or tree opposite, it will never dance with sunshine. So any effects that have sunny associations – cane furniture, fresh, spriggy flower and summertime stencil motifs – will lose some of their

impact. Of course, lack of natural light in dark rooms can be compensated for in part by clever effects with artificial light, but a useful old decorating tenet is that if you have a dark room, paint it dark. This need not mean that it will be gloomy. In a north-facing room, make the most of deep, rich colours such as russet, Pompeian red, terracotta, darkest green, burnt umber. These colours can become hard and garish in bright sunshine, but they are in their element when direct sunlight is kept at bay.

AWKWARD CEILINGS

A room that has very high ceilings can easily be given better proportions by the addition of a stencilled picture rail and/or a dado rail. You can add further interest by including panels or a more elaborate stencil pattern below the dado rail, to contrast with the plainer wall space above, or vice versa. Paint the

ceiling a darker colour than the walls to make it seem lower than it is in reality. And lower it further again if you wish by taking this darker colour down to the picture rail. This will also have the advantage of 'containing' your stencil design and showing it off to the best effect.

Just as high ceilings can be made to seem lower by using dark colours, so low ceilings become taller when they are painted a shade that is lighter than that of the walls. Ceilings that are painted pale or white colours also reflect the maximum amount of light. Use narrow, vertical stencil designs on the walls to lead the eye upwards and try to limit yourself to low-level furnishings so that

The addition of stencil details, which can be as simple or complex as you wish, improves the proportions of even the most ordinary room.

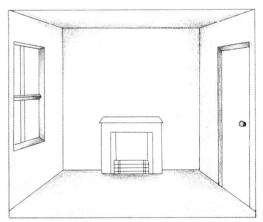

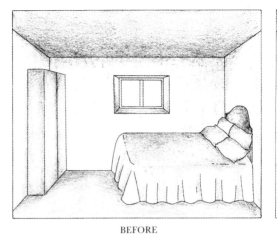

BEFORE

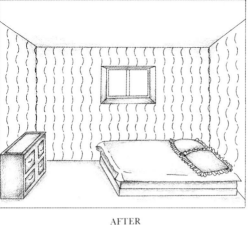

AFTER

The use of low furnishings, vertical stencil patterns and a pale ceiling colour will create the illusion of extra height in a room with a low ceiling.

the wall space is given as much emphasis as possible.

If you have a room with a sloping ceiling and you want to make a special feature of it, you can draw it into your scheme for the walls by using an individual stencil motif that extends to the ceiling and leads the eye upwards. Alternatively, you may emphasize the slope by running a wide, stencilled border along it at the point where the wall meets the ceiling. A frieze that has movement in it can be very effective in this context. Decide which part of the room you want to draw attention to and place the stencil so that it leads the eye in this direction: if you have a bathroom with a pretty view from the window in the lower wall, you could have a border of waves tumbling down towards the window. Or, if the

main feature is an interesting old mirror on the higher wall, you could run a climbing ivy stencil up the slope and even weave it around the mirror itself.

THE BORING BOX

Don't despair if your bedroom or sitting room is a plain box with no redeeming architectural features. Remember that as soon as you introduce furniture it will be transformed. Break up the monotony of the room by stencilling an exuberant design on one or two of the walls only, to contrast with the other, plainer two. Divide the walls into panels of varying sizes. If you are feeling adventurous, create a *trompe l'oeil* vista through an imaginary door or window.

IRREGULAR SURFACES

Irregular surfaces are murderous to wallpaperers, but a joy for stencil artists. The lumps and bumps speak of simple, rough-and-ready workmanship and invite naive, unsophisticated designs that

Give life to a boring, box-shaped room by stencilling a border round the window, making this the focal point. Introduce a strong design on one or two of the other walls to add further character.

BEFORE

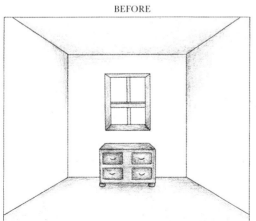

AFTER

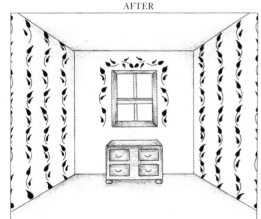

will harmonize quietly with the quirks of uneven plasterwork in old farmhouses and cottages. Avoid geometric designs; instead choose a simple, individual stencil motif to be repeated at random across the walls. If you are good at judging distances by eye, don't be afraid to apply the stencil without measuring up; any irregularities will be in keeping with the surface on which you are working. Do measure up if you are unsure of yourself, but remember that uneven surfaces defy precise measurement, so don't expect a perfectly balanced and symmetrical result.

TOO MUCH WALL

Large, double-reception rooms or open-plan rooms can be intimidating, and though the luxury of space is highly prized by most of us, it can make a room seem empty and lacking in atmosphere. Be bold! If you have a lot of wall space you can go to town in the filling of it. Itsy-bitsy flower borders and dainty motifs will be lost in a large expanse of space. Big rooms invite big designs. Vertical patterns will come into their own — the bigger the better if you want to 'fill' the room and pull it together. Framing the design in a series of stencilled panels will lend further interest and break up the room in an unobtrusive way. This is particularly helpful if you want to use a room for two or more purposes — dining in one corner, sofas for flopping into round the fireplace, limbo dancing or whatever in the bay window. . .

NARROW SPACES

Corridors, cloakrooms, stairways and bathrooms are often all too conspicuously narrow and functional — not much fun as rooms in themselves. But these spaces harbour hidden possibilities: run bookcases or shelves along the far wall of a cloakroom and enliven the others with stencils in a bold, diamond trellis pattern; create a tiled wall or stencilled panels to dado height to break the height of walls in a confined space; use mirrors at the far end of a passage to catch the colours of the room it leads into and invite the visitor to venture further; paint the far wall of any narrow room with warm, dark colours and stencils to make it seem closer, or with pale colours if you want to enlarge the space by making the end wall seem further away; break up a long passage with a softly draped curtain

Two possible treatments that give interest and purpose to a narrow space.

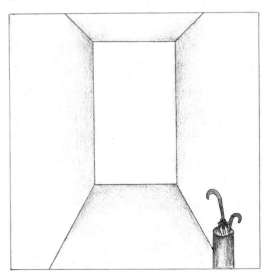

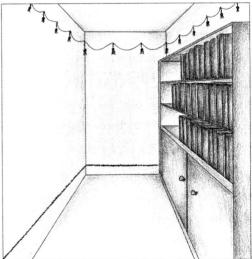

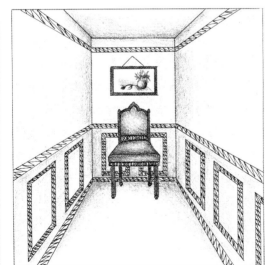

and use one stencil design at one side of the curtain and a different one beyond.

L-shaped rooms

L-shaped rooms lend themselves to being split and used for two purposes. Emphasize that division by demarcating the shorter part of the L with a pair of stencilled columns or pillars if you want an aura of grandeur or, if you prefer, with two plain panels that contain a stencil motif added on top of the background colour. If you have used a simple stencil motif in the larger part of the room, intensify this in the smaller part to create contrast and a feeling of warmth and intimacy without divorcing the two parts of the room from each other. Thus, a floral border in the main section of an L-shaped room can be used more densely, and with more colourways, in the smaller section of the room.

Problem Furniture

If you are a first-time homemaker and are making regular forays for furniture from auction rooms, furniture stores and secondhand junk shops, as well as decorating from scratch, you will be free to buy furniture that complements your overall plans, rather than the other way around. Alternatively, you may be rich and reckless enough to discard and replace your furniture as and when you feel like it. But if, like the majority of people, you don't fit into either of these categories, you will need to bear in mind the colour, size and shape of your armchairs, beds, carpets and other furnishings if you are to avoid walls that clash with chairs that clash with curtains that clash with dogbasket.

In this context, stencilling has a head and shoulders advantage over other forms of interior decoration. Pick out a motif on a favourite bedspread, make a stencil using the same motif and use it to adorn plain bedside and dressing table lampshades and painted bedroom chairs. Does your child have a favourite teddy bear? Then give the teddy company in the form of a teddy-bear frieze running round his nursery; buy cheap chintz curtain fabric and stencil teddies on that too. If you have inherited an exquisite piece of chinoiserie that is the pride of your drawing room, extend the oriental theme with colours and stencils that convey the mystery and exoticism of the east. If, on the other hand, your partner, spouse or flatmate cannot live without (you and) an enormous, shabby tallboy that threatens to swallow up your sitting room, pull out your stencil box to temper its impact. A lick of paint and a delicate fern or leaf stencil, or a subtle geometric pattern, can transform the ugliest of artefacts. And again, you can repeat the design in door-panels or round a mantelpiece; though you may feel you've done your duty simply by making the monstrous object

The trailing leaves and flowers of Myrickview make an attractive contrast to this cast-iron fireplace.

The natural stone of this mantlepiece is echoed in the beautifully subtle colours of the wall stencil.

into one that you both find live-with-able.

And, if you do have furniture that needs a facelift, as well as walls, floors and ceilings to decorate, work out your priorities. It costs a great deal less to stencil than to wallpaper a room, so if you have money to spare and you hate or have had enough of the chintz on your sofas, first choose the stencil design you think will look best on the walls, then seek out the fabric that will complement it and have the furniture reupholstered. It will look as good as new and you will be much happier not to have had to compromise. Don't be afraid to combine old and new: your old kitchen table and chairs may look rather sorry for them-

David Mendel designed and painted this stencil for Francis Burne using the pattern of the curtains for inspiration.

selves on tacky linoleum, but a jaunty, stencilled floorcloth will liven them up considerably. And you will find that you are no longer ashamed to have your great-aunt's armchairs in the same room as your new sofabed if all the pieces are brightened up with welcoming piles of stencilled cushions.

PICTURES

'I have a predilection for painting that lends joyousness to a room,' said Renoir. Good paintings do just that, and to do so at their best they should be hung against appropriate backgrounds. Pictures need to be seen. This may sound like an obvious statement, but it is surprising how many people hang pictures against riotous wallpaper designs, with the result that they become insignificant. If you have a picture that you don't like, sell it. If you like the image, but not the mount or frame, have the mount and/or frame changed or get rid of them altogether and simply hang the painting behind protective glass.

Whatever option you choose, make sure that your pictures hang against a background that will do justice to them. Off-white is a safe bet for most pictures and wallhangings, but other colours can be very dramatic and effective. Dark oil paintings look impressive against rich yellows, reds and greens. Watercolours need more delicate pastel tones, as do

line drawings. Small pictures with wide mounts can benefit from the addition of a stencilled outer frame in colours that complement those of the image itself.

If you want to show off a collection of prints to the best advantage, you can't do better than to create a contemporary print room with *trompe l'oeil* stencil ropes and ribbons. You will find examples of print rooms in Part II, and full instructions on how to design your own in Part III.

It can be fun to smother a wall with an eclectic mixture of paintings and prints. In that case, don't bother to stencil the wall in question; save your energies for more visible areas. Your stencils should be a feast for the eye; so too should your pictures. By deciding beforehand what you will hang where, your stencilling and your picture-hanging will each enhance the other and combine fluently to give you endless visual pleasure.

ATMOSPHERE

You have thought about the problems your room poses, and how to tackle them; you have thought about some if not all of the furniture that will live there. Now you need to think about the atmosphere you would like to create. To some extent, this will be determined by the function of the room, the type of house you live in, and your domestic circumstances. A nursery is the ideal place in which to use bright primary colours and naïve designs. Together, these will create a cheerful, sunny atmosphere with lots of eye-catching elements to capture the attention of your children and their friends. Subtle understatements are out of place here. Some adults may appreciate minimalist design but children are bored by it. How much use does your main reception room get? If you are host to a constant stream of visitors, or if you are one of a large household, you may find it difficult to maintain too formal an atmosphere and opt instead for a more comfortable and casual ambiance. Equally, you may long to preserve at least one room in the house as a sanctuary of civilization and decide to create a room that speaks of quiet sophistication and discreetly classical good taste.

Reflect on the mood that you wish to awaken in yourself and others who will use the room. Do you want to be impressively grand or invitingly scruffy? Do you want minimal, bare ascetic surroundings or welcoming heaps of rugs, books,

ABOVE: *Deep, rich reds with gilded stencils designed by Alidad Mahloudji, from Alidad Ltd, make this very much a room for evening entertaining.*
BOTTOM LEFT AND RIGHT: *Pale and dark walls create completely different, but equally effective, atmospheres for stencils.*

© Stencil-Ease® USA.

cushions, clutter? If you have the luxury of a dining room that can be used simply for dining, it is worth creating dramatic background effects that will be enhanced by candlelight. But you will probably not want to live with the same colours and textures if the same room has to double each morning as a breakfast room. It can be fun to play decorative jokes in houses, but the jokes can start to aggravate if you are constantly reminded of them. So don't create an ingenious three-dimensional *trompe l'oeil* in your one and only sitting room if you will have to sit and look at it every evening. Save it instead for a dull corridor or landing, an occasionally used study or a spare bedroom or bathroom. However, whatever mood you want to achieve, don't be afraid of adventure. One of the great assets of stencils is that they are quickly and easily applied, and they can be just as quickly and easily retouched or painted out. So if you do tire of a particular creation after a few months, you will only need a few spare hours to transform the room once more into a place that offers new delights.

Colour

The one factor that will do more than anything else to establish the mood and character of your room is your use of colour. Picture one of your favourite rooms in your mind's eye. What do you remember most clearly about it? As likely as not, your clearest memory will be its colour. 'The purest and most thoughtful minds are those which love colour most,' wrote Ruskin. We all love colour of course, but some of us may be less conscious of it than we realise. From the earliest times, we have learnt to use colour in myriad ways to capture, celebrate and enjoy the fleeting qualities of what we perceive around us. Across the centuries, artists, illustrators, portraitists and designers have all developed techniques in the creation of colour to express their particular genius, to show others the beauty of what they see or imagine, and to reflect the passing tastes, fashions and enthusiasms of their particular era. Colour talks and each shade, each texture, each combination of colour talks in its own individual way. The same artist working in colour pastels will create an entirely different painting to the one that will result from his working on an identical subject in oils.

These differences also apply to the interior decorator. If you cover your walls with a standard, commercial paint and apply stencils to this surface, the result will be very different to that you would achieve if you mixed your own glaze and dragged or ragged the walls before stencilling. Both treatments have their charms; which one you choose will depend on your taste and to some extent on your skills. But don't be deterred from tackling special paint finishes for fear that they can only be achieved successfully by experts; with a little practice and dexterity, some very exciting paint effects are well within the reach of any enthusiastic amateur.

THE LANGUAGE OF COLOUR

Everyone loves colour, but not everyone knows how to use it. To a large extent, use of colour is instinctive. But if you feel underconfident about your colour sense and are afraid of making horrible mistakes with the colour schemes in your home, it is well worth while learning some basic rules about the language and behaviour of colour:

Primary colours
These, as every schoolchild learns, are:
   red
   yellow
   blue

Secondary colours
The combination of any two primary colours produces the secondary colours:
   red + blue = purple
   red + yellow = orange
   blue + yellow = green

Tertiary colours
Similarly, combining a primary and a secondary colour, or combining two secondary colours, produces a tertiary colour:

orange + purple = russett
blue + green = turquoise
orange + red = terracotta
red + purple = magenta

Black and white
The addition of white to any colour creates a tint, while the addition of black to any colour creates a shade. If you are mixing a pale colour, white will be the dominant element in the mixture. Add the colour of your choice little by little, stirring each addition well in. You will only need to add about 5 per cent of the colour you wish to tint for quite a powerful result. Similarly, just a splash of black will create a darker shade of the colour you are working with. And in both cases, a hint of brown in the mixture will give it a special depth and subtlety — it is for this reason that raw umber takes pride of place in the paint collection of any professional decorator.

Note how different a design can look when the same colour combination is reversed.

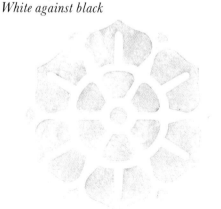

Black against white

White against black

Coal Black

Coal Black tinted with Moonlight White

Moonlight White shaded with Coal Black

COLOUR VALUES

Any colour can be mixed with white, black or another colour to create a darker or lighter effect. The intensity of the resulting tint or shade is that colour's value. If two colours are to combine harmoniously, they have to be of the same value. Thus, pale pink and pale blue elephants will look happy together in a frieze around a nursery, but if the pink is too bright, the blue will be overpowered and the frieze will look unbalanced.

COMBINING COLOURS

Most of us have favourite colours that we tend to choose when buying clothes or decorating our homes. But the same colour used in excess can be both overpowering and difficult to live with. If you step out in a green hat, green coat and matching green shoes, your outfit will look uniform but lifeless. Exchange the green hat for a red one with a green ribbon, add red buttons to the coat, kick off the green shoes and slip into a pair of scarlet ones and you'll start turning heads. Why? Because red complements green. A complementary colour brings its opposite to life. So if you use complementary colours when you are stencilling, you can be confident that you are creating a room that is both lively and 'easy on the eye'. Remember too that the background colour you choose will affect the value of the colours that are stencilled

Stencil-Ease's® Spring Bouquet is manufactured as a two-colour stencil. However, you can also use it as a single colour or multi-colour design. The same motif creates completely different effects when used with these different colour combinations.

over it. It isn't difficult to predict the result of stencilling onto a light background, but when you stencil onto a medium or dark background this will show through the stencil paint and affect its colour. Dark backgrounds can be very attractive and original, but it is worth experimenting with your colour combinations before you start so that you have an idea of what the final effect will be like.

WARM AND COLD COLOURS

We all respond, whether consciously or unconsciously, to colour. If you look at pink cherry blossom against a grey sky, it will affect you in a different way to looking at white apple blossom against a blue sky, not just because the weather is different but also because the colours are different. How many times have you been in a drab office or railway station and thought 'what this place needs is a good lick of paint'? In other words, what you thought was that it needed a good lick of colour.

Colour has been proven to have a psychological influence over us, and various colours have been categorized according to the effects they induce. The two most obvious categories are warm and cold colours. Red and its derivatives create a feeling of warmth, whilst blues create a cooler atmosphere.

It is important to bear these distinctions in mind when you are decorating a room. If you have a cold, gloomy back bedroom and you want to change it into a warm, cosy television room, don't paint it Prussian blue. By the same token, you should resist strong reds, oranges and rusts in a room that enjoys a lot of sun — otherwise you will feel as if you are living in an inferno!

RED

Red is bold, bright, intense and provokes an immediate response. Its impact is so powerful that it needs careful handling — red walls cannot be combined with too many other bright patterns and furnishing fabrics. Among the most popular reds are scarlet, flame, terracotta, burgundy, raspberry, magenta and coral. Use your favourite shade in a room where you can afford to reduce the wall space, and where you want to create a sense of richness and drama. This effect will be further intensified if you introduce black or darkest grey stencil designs. It will be made fresher and more informal if you choose blue stencils.

YELLOW

The colour of the life-giving sun, yellow is also the colour of optimism. In confined spaces, bright yellows give a sense of openness and light, and at the same time introduce a feeling of warmth. The paler yellows, such as peach, sand and primrose, are perennially popular for their unobtrusive restfulness and their ability to increase the amount of light in gloomy rooms. All yellows make ideal companions to natural woods. They also have a great affinity to the green shades and the bright yellows look striking with white. You will achieve a quite different, though equally pleasing, effect by combining yellow with blue.

BLUE

Despite its position as a cold colour in the colour spectrum, blue can be unrivalled for creating an atmosphere of peace and tranquillity. The middle range of blues — cobalt, cornflower blue, sky blue — are the easiest to work with when creating a room with a serene, calming influence. They also combine most effectively with palest pastels such as pink, peach, cream and pale grey. Blue is best used as a background colour on walls in rooms which receive a fair amount of sun.

PURPLE

This powerful secondary colour has a long history of association with royalty, formality and grandeur. All of the purples speak of distinction and elegance, and the pale shades — violet, lilac, lavender — are recognized as inducing a contemplative and tranquil frame of mind. Lavender enjoyed great popularity in the past and is a beautiful foil for the delicate, refined furnishings of the eighteenth century. Rooms that receive little natural light, and are therefore used in the evening rather than during the day, can be made strikingly dramatic with the darker purples.

GREEN

Perhaps more than any other colour, green is surrounded with superstition, and as a result regarded with ambivalence by many people. Yet it is one of the most reliable colours for the interior decorator, partly because of its neutral qualities, which make it a perfect, unobtrusive background colour, and partly because it can combine successfully with any other colour. Strong, bright greens such as jade, emerald and leaf green contrast dramatically with white woodwork and also make excellent backdrops for oil paintings. The pale greens create an air of restfulness and are cool without being as cold as corresponding shades of blue.

HOW TO PLAN A SUCCESSFUL COLOUR SCHEME

Successful stencilling draws a room together and gives it that final definition and finish to which anyone aspires who cares about his or her surroundings. The elements that contribute to this end result go beyond a happy combination of stencil and surface, of balance, position and proportion. Every item that is in a room makes a contribution to that room's character. In general, however, the main elements that establish the particular character of any room are the walls and floor, the main pieces of furniture and the window treatment. Professional decorators are particularly conscious of this and they deal with it by preparing room samples for their clients' consideration before they start work. Unfortunately, it is all but impossible to imagine exactly what the final effect of a decorative scheme will be like before you have started, but you will find that you greatly reduce the risk of making mistakes if you prepare similar samples for yourself.

Standard manufacturer's samples bring together all the dominant elements that will set the character of the room in question. They comprise the paints that are under consideration for walls, woodwork and ceiling, the curtain or blind fabric, the upholstery fabric and the intended flooring. So, when you are planning your stencilling scheme, do not only experiment with different stencils against different background paint surfaces, but extend your experimenting by making samples which will enable you to assess the effectiveness of your schemes in relation to these other essential components. It's fun! You will probably find that you start to flirt with colour combinations that you had not initially considered and you may be quite surprised by your reactions to different combinations of colour, shape and pattern. In many ways, stencilling is similar to dressmaking: the time you spend at the sewing machine is usually far less than the time spent selecting the right pattern and the right material and cutting out the design. If you want to create truly magical stencil effects, do pay attention to these primary decorating principles.

BEFORE AND AFTER

Before: a room — maybe a house — which, whether you want to change completely or simply add an extra, personal touch to, is not entirely to your liking. After: if all goes well, a home which will delight you for many years. Between these two states you will have spent many hours exploring, experimenting and creating, and when your work is done you will probably already have forgotten what the room was like before you started. It is well worth while taking photographs before you start and as you progress, as well as recording the final result. It will be fun for you to look back and remember the place as it used to be, and to compare it with what it is like in its new state. It will also be useful to show the photographs to estate agents or prospective buyers if you ever plan to move, as an indication of the improvements you have made to your property. And, commercial considerations apart, nothing is more pleasing than to have decorated a room, a flat, a mansion or a farmhouse in such a fashion that it carries the stamp of your own taste and personality and creates an ambiance which gives equal pleasure to your family and your friends.

BEFORE

ABOVE: *After five years, the green and white walls in the bedroom of my previous London flat were looking tired, but I could not justify a total change of furnishings.*

AFTER

RIGHT: *My solution was to give the room a new lease of life by repapering the walls with a pale peach Osborne and Little rag-look paper that picked up a different colour in the fabrics. I completed the transformation by stencilling the 1811 House design around the walls and cupboards.*

TWO

SURFACE PREPARATION

WHATEVER you plan to stencil, whether it be a small object or the walls and floor of a room, it is absolutely vital that the surface you choose is suitable for stencilling. Fortunately, most surfaces are. Once they have been prepared and given time to dry, you can stencil directly onto: lampshades; floorcloths and baskets; matt wallpapers; emulsion [latex], flat oil-based or mid-sheen, oil-based paint surfaces; bare, stained, bleached or painted wood; glazed paint surfaces; tinware and leather. If you are stencilling on fabric, choose a plain cotton or linen. Synthetic fibres, wool and textured cloth are not recommended. Wash your fabric and, when it is dry, iron out the creases before stencilling.

Unless you use specialist ceramic paints, you cannot guarantee satisfactory results if stencilling onto anything that has a shiny or slick surface. This includes high-gloss paint, ceramics, vinyls,

linoleum, glass and mirrors. Nor would we advise that you stencil onto unpainted wall surfaces such as plasterboard and sheetrock. If the surface you intend to stencil is in poor condition, do take the trouble to prepare it properly. Walls, floors, furniture and tinware that are not in the right state can all be prepared in a number of different ways, and the option you choose will depend to some extent on the character of the surface and on the effect you want to achieve.

If you are undertaking a major project that will require a lot of foundation work, you may well prefer to have professional decorators do the basic preparation for you. An understanding of the elementary rules for treating walls and woodwork will help you to give a clear brief and to monitor the work to ensure that the result is what you intended. If you plan to do everything yourself, the following guidelines will take you through the necessary

stages of preparing wall surfaces, woodwork and tinware so that they are suitable for stencilling. We shall not go into great detail on the many special glaze finishes that are possible, as there are a large number of books on the market which explain at length how to master the necessary techniques for achieving such effects. However, we shall describe the best-known of these techniques so that you have the basic information you need if you want to restore or decorate a room or piece of furniture from scratch.

Stencilling combines with a variety of other decorative finishes to give special interest to the corner of this room. The table, which is a cheap junk shop buy, has been cleverly marblized, dragged and stencilled with Easy Peasy. Easy Peasy also gives definition to the ragged and dragged trompe l'oeil wall panels.

PREPARING WALLS

Wall surfaces that are unpainted, that have been painted or wallpapered in colours that are not to your taste or that have been painted with a high-gloss paint, need to be suitably prepared before you start stencilling:

NEW PLASTER

New plaster must be given time to dry out completely before you start to decorate. When it is dry, apply one coat of sealer — choose one that will stop salts and fungi penetrating the paintwork or paper to be applied.

WALLPAPER

Measure up your wallspace, select a good-quality matt wallpaper and hang according to the manufacturer's instructions.

PAINT

1. Again, measure your wallspace and consult your paint retailer about the quantities you will need.
2. Apply a white undercoat of mid-sheen, oil-based paint or matt emulsion [latex].
3. Sand lightly to remove any irregularities.
4. Apply the first coat of your chosen paint colour.
5. Sand lightly again.
6. Apply the second coat of your chosen paint colour.
7. If you prefer a textured effect, you can apply the paint with a roller and leave the surface unsanded. Remember that it is best not to use high-gloss paint.

GLAZE

1. Apply a coat of white, mid-sheen, oil-based paint.
2. Sand lightly to remove any irregularities.
3. Apply the first coat of your chosen base colour. Again this should be a mid-sheen, oil-based paint.
4. Sand lightly again.
5. Apply the second coat of your chosen base colour.

OLD PLASTER

Any cracks and holes in old plaster should be patched up using all-purpose filler. Give the treated areas plenty of time to dry and sand them down before proceeding as for new plaster, though in this case you need only apply sealer to the areas you have filled.

WALLS IN POOR CONDITION

Many old houses have walls that have deteriorated to such an extent that the plasterwork is a maze of cracks. If this is the case, fill the cracks as well as you can, sand them down, and then hang them with a good quality lining paper which will conceal the evidence beneath. Once the paper has dried out thoroughly, apply a coat of emulsion [latex] paint thinned down with an added 10 per cent of clean water to seal the porous surface of the lining paper and prevent any wooliness from showing up. Then follow the instructions given for new plaster.

Some old houses have rooms which have been decorated with several successive layers of wallpaper, behind which lies plasterwork which could well crumble and disintegrate if the paper were to be stripped away. If you are worried that this might happen, sand down any irregularities in the seams of the wallpaper to stop them showing through, then follow the instructions given for new plaster on this page.

GLAZING WALLS

Glazing is undergoing a well-deserved revival as a decorative technique. A glaze is essentially a transparent layer of colour, and the application of successive layers of the same or of different colours will create an extraordinary illusion of many dimensions. No commercial paint or wallpaper can match the depth and subtlety of colour that gives glazed surfaces their particular magic. Oil-glaze techniques include ragging, dragging, flogging, sponging, stippling, combing and cross-brushing. Of these, sponging and ragging are the easiest for the amateur decorator; the others require a fair degree of dexterity with the paintbrush, a steady hand and the ability to work at a reasonable speed. In each case, the success of the end result also depends on the skill with which the colours are selected. For the dedicated enthusiast, the possibilities are endless.

Commercially prepared glaze is known as scumble glaze, and if you are new to glazing it is best to use this rather than making your own. You will also need a selection of artists' oil paints to mix the colour of your choice. Start by blending the oil paints with a little turpentine until you have the colour you require. This is a matter of trial and error — do persist until you are happy with the result. As a rule of thumb, mix tertiary colours if you want to maximize the illusion of depth —

primary and secondary colours give a brighter, flatter result. Once you have the blend you want, add the basic scumble glaze little by little to the colour until you have the quantity you require. Ask your retailer's advice on the quantities you will need for the room you want to glaze, and ensure you mix all you need before you start, as colours are difficult to match. Mix the glaze the day before you need it so that the colours have time to settle and amalgamate. Make sure that the room in which you are working is free from dust and leave a window open to disperse the fumes of the glaze. Remember too that oil glaze dries slowly. On dry summer days, your work should dry within twenty-four hours, but in damp conditions this time should be doubled. Always remember to dispose of glaze-coated rags safely to avoid fire risk, following the manufacturer's directions.

SPONGING

To sponge a room, you will need a natural sea sponge. Invest in two if you want to use both hands — this will enable you to progress quickly and create a natural result.

1. Start at the ceiling and brush on the glaze, working downwards to the skirting board across an area of approximately 3 ft (1 metre).
2. Now wet the sponge in your glaze mixture and wring it out so that it is damp but not dripping. Pat the

sponge gently against the wall surface, taking care that you do not allow too much glaze to build up on the sponge. To prevent this from happening, blot the sponge regularly on a paper towel.
3. Work in this way round the room, stopping regularly to monitor your progress and retouch the glaze if necessary.
4. Leave the glaze to dry for at least a day before stencilling. Allow two days if the weather is humid.

To maximize the impact of sponging, apply two or more successive layers of glaze, allowing time for each to dry. A succession of subtly different shades of colour will create a beautiful result.

RAGGING AND RAG-ROLLING

Ragging and rag-rolling are the quickest and easiest ways of creating a glaze of considerable character and impact. Choose soft muttoncloth for a discreet, parchment result; cheesecloth will give a more textured surface; stiff cotton is best for a harder, bolder edge. It is fun to experiment with a variety of cloths before you start but, as a general rule, soft fabrics create a surface that is more compatible with stencils than stiff materials.

1. Apply the glaze, working from the ceiling down to the skirting board to a width of approximately 3 ft (1 metre).

2. Now wet your cloth and wring it out so that it is damp but not dripping.

3. Working downwards, pat the cloth gently against the glaze. Take care to blot the cloth regularly on a paper towel so that it does not build up too much glaze.

4. Continue round the room, working strip by strip and checking your work at regular intervals so that you can retouch it where necessary before the glaze dries.

To rag-roll, follow these instructions but wind up your cloth into a tight roll, hold it at either end and work downwards as if you were using a rolling pin.

As with sponging, ragged glaze should be left for at least twenty-four hours to dry before stencilling, and for forty-eight hours in humid conditions.

DRAGGING AND STIPPLING

Instructions for dragging and stippling are described under the section on preparing woodwork (see page 37). If you want to drag or stipple a wall, read those instructions for guidance on brush technique and proceed by working downwards in strips of 3 ft (1 metre) wide, as described under sponging. For more comprehensive glazing instructions, consult the Bibliography on page 178. However, if you find that you become a real glaze enthusiast, the best way to improve is simply by practice. An ounce of practice is worth a ton of theory!

FLOORS

Before you stencil a floor, you must remove all trace of the previous finish by machine sanding. It is best to have this done professionally — dust will go everywhere and unless you are experienced you will find it difficult to achieve an even grain. However, ask your floor sander not to create too smooth a finish — if the surface is at all shiny it will not take paints or stains well.

Once the old finish has been removed, make sure all of the dust in the room is cleared before you proceed. Don't stencil direct onto the bare wood or you will run the risk of having your designs bleed into the surface. If you want to retain the look of the wood as it is, use a matt sealer to stop the stencil paint from running. Alternatively, you can bleach, paint or glaze the floor before applying your stencil design.

BLEACHING

To bleach a floor well requires a good knowledge of different types of wood. If you follow this option, it is best to enlist the services of a professional. After the floor has been bleached, sand it lightly as the bleaching process will have raised the grain of the wood.

STAINING

You should stain your floor if you want the grain and knots to play a part in your

The stencilled floor design of this hall echoes the natural curves of the room and shows off the quality of the woodwork.

Hand-stencilled and colour-washed floor tiles made from medium density fibreboard and protected with several coats of polyester resin

overall design. A wide variety of stains are available through paint and hardware stores and DIY shops. Of these, the most suitable for floors which are to be stencilled are the oil-based stains which are the least prone to streaking and also penetrate, seal and protect the wood. If you don't like any of the ready-mixed blends, add artists' oil paints until you have the colour you are happy with. As with glazes, the mixture should be made in advance and left to settle. Apply two coats with a wide brush, allowing plenty of time for each layer to dry.

PAINTING

The process for painting a floor is exactly the same as for painting walls. Don't neglect to sand down the surface after each application or the raised grain will disrupt your stencilling. And don't forget that gloss paint must not be used. Choose a flat oil-based paint or a mid-sheen, oil-based paint.

GLAZING

The same rules apply for preparing floors as for preparing walls:

1. Apply a white, mid-sheen, oil-based undercoat, leave to dry and sand down to remove any irregularities.
2. Apply the first coat of your chosen base colour and repeat the sanding process.
3. Apply the second coat of your chosen

base colour and lightly sand down once more.

When you are stencilling a floor, it is very important to take the trouble to measure up before you start. Detailed instructions for this are given in Part III (page 163).

WOODWORK

Doors, skirting boards, bookcases, chests, windowframes, bath panels, furniture and boxes are all excellent candidates for stencilling. Whatever you choose, you can start work immediately provided the surface is stained with a non-gloss finish, painted with a flat or mid-sheen, oil-based paint, or bleached and sealed. If you don't like the finish of the woodwork you intend to stencil, strip it off using a commercial paint stripper. This is a laborious process for large pieces of furniture and these are best sent to a specialist where they can be dipped as a whole into vats of stripper. As with floors, the wood can then be painted, stained, bleached or glazed and the same instructions apply. If you want to drag or stipple a wooden surface, apply three successive layers of mid-sheen, oil-based paint as described under wall glazes (page 34). Read the outline instructions for glaze techniques and apply the glaze as follows:

STIPPLING

The ideal tool for stippling is a bristle

SOME WAYS OF STENCILLING ON WOOD

A marblized architrave contains Alex Davidson's elaborate stencil designs taken from Islamic motifs which have been applied onto a painted wooden door panel.

The discreet use of Cordelia Border gives distinction to a painted radiator casing.

Stencil details on dragged woodwork and sponged walls.

extremely expensive. They are worth investing in if you are planning to drag a considerable area, otherwise use an ordinary 6-in (15-cm) paintbrush.

— Apply the glaze working from the top of the object downwards. Glaze a small area at a time.
— Dip the brush into the glaze mix, then dab off most of it on to a paper towel, leaving the tips damp and slightly splayed.
— Hold the brush as steadily as you can and drag it down through the glaze with a quick, clean movement. Try to maintain the same pressure as you work.
— Work round all the surfaces until the object is finished, checking for drips and dribbles as you progress.

stippling brush. These are not cheap, however. For small objects, you can achieve a perfectly good result with a nylon-bristled paint brush.

— Apply the glaze, working first over the top of the item you have chosen. If you are stippling a door or windowframe, start at the top and work downwards.
— Use a light, tapping movement to stipple the glaze, taking care to hold the brush at a right angle to the surface so that the stipples do not become smears.

— Check your work for drips and dribbles, especially if you are working on curved chair or table legs and mouldings where the glaze will tend to accumulate.
— Allow to dry thoroughly before stencilling.

DRAGGING

Dragging is the most difficult of all glaze techniques to perfect. However, don't let this deter you! As long as you are not too ambitious with projects, there is no reason why you should not achieve good results. Professional dragging brushes are

CERAMICS

It is not advisable to stencil ceramic surfaces such as tiles, vases, *cache-pots*, lampstands and ornamental ceramics using standard stencil paints. If you want to stencil a ceramic surface, you would do well to invest in the specially formulated Ceramic à Froid paints that are sold from our London shop, and from specialist paint stores. It will not be worth your while to stencil items such as plates that are used on a regular basis as the design is likely to be damaged in no time at all.

Ceramic paints are durable, but their use is best confined to decorative items. Remember:

— Wipe the ceramic surface with white spirit and leave it to dry.
— Wear rubber gloves to stencil as ceramic paint is difficult to wash off bare hands.
— Secure the stencil to the ceramic surface with masking tape and follow the instructions given in Chapter 3, but remember that ceramic paint is not fast-drying.
— Seal the stencilled surface with clear gloss varnish or polyeurethane.

TINWARE

Tinware makes a good stencilling surface, provided it has been properly prepared and treated with a couple of coats of oil-based paint. Because many tinware items can be picked up relatively cheaply, they make good objects for newcomers to stencilling — old biscuit tins being the most obvious candidates. Proceed as follows:

1. Remove any rust from the tin with a rust remover. Wash with soap and warm water and leave to dry.
2. Sand the surfaces smooth if necessary.
3. Apply a metal primer to protect the tin from rusting in the future.

4. Apply the first coat of mid-sheen, oil-based paint.
5. Sand down any irregularities.
6. Apply the second coat of paint.
7. Sand down again.
8. Proceed to stencil following the standard instructions in Chapter 3.

BRONZING

Bronzing with stencils is a cheap and easy way of transforming walls, woodwork, furniture and fabrics. It was originally conceived by early American craftsmen to emulate the ornate but, for the early pioneers, prohibitively expensive gilded work in gold and silver leaf that was so popular in Europe. Inevitably, the skill recrossed the Atlantic and bronzing became a major form of decoration in Europe and America during the Empire period.

Today, bronzing can be used as a stencilling technique with a recently formulated range of lustre paints and bronzing powders from Stencil-Ease.® The collection includes a wide selection of bronzing powders, among them gold, copper, silver, sapphire blues, emerald greens and ruby reds. You can produce endless colour variations by mixing and matching these colour ranges. The bronzing powders need to be mixed with gold, silver or pearl 'lustre' paints before being applied, as follows:

1. Pour a tiny amount of bronzing powder onto a scrap of velvet or other soft fabric.
2. Dip your stencil brush lightly into a jar of lustre paint.
3. Dip the brush into the bronzing powder and mix with the paint.
4. Wipe off any excess onto a paper towel.
5. Proceed to stencil following the standard instructions in Chapter 3.

Lustre paints mixed with bronzing powders must be used immediately and cannot be stored for future projects.

These bronzing powders cannot be mixed with any paint except Stencil-Ease's® lustre paints.

Stencil-Ease's® lustre paints and bronzing powders can be used to great effect on painted furniture and other items as well as on walls.

THREE

HOW TO STENCIL

PROVIDED the surface you intend to work on is in the right condition, no elaborate preparation is needed before you embark on a stencilling project. But don't try to squeeze the work in between coming home from your office and dashing out to a dinner party. Give yourself plenty of time and prepare to have fun. Choose a time of day when there is lots of natural light in the room where you are working. Clear the room of as much furniture as possible and protect any that remains with dust sheets, dustbin bags or old newspapers. Make sure that the surfaces you plan to stencil are clean and that they have had time to dry before you begin.

STENCILLING EQUIPMENT

STENCILS

If you are new to stencilling you will probably find it easiest to buy ready-made, pre-cut designs for your early pro-

jects. There are now hundreds of designs on the world market. Of these, our London shop stocks a unique selection of over two hundred designs from many leading manfacturers. In theory, stencils can be cut out of any durable, flexible material — in the past, these have included paper, pasteboard, oilcloth and leather. Nowadays, commercially produced stencils are available in oiled manila board and in transparent plastic. If the design is un-cut, you will need a sharp craft knife, a cutting board and a steady hand to cut out the design before you can start to stencil. The most obvious disadvantage of this method for the novice is that it can be very tricky to cut neatly enough to ensure a clean, straight edge, and of course one slip of the knife can damage the card. Of the pre-cut stencils available, those printed on card can be diffi-cult to use on areas where the stencil has to be bent, and the stenciller cannot see

through the opaque card to check that the design is not becoming smudged or smeared. Pre-cut plastic stencils, on the other hand, are transparent so that the stenciller can see exactly what is happen-ing as he or she progresses. Unlike card stencils, pre-cut plastic stencils also have printed instructions and repeat marks which spare you the painstaking task of lining up every motif as you move the stencil along the surface upon which you are working.

PAINT

If you have never stencilled before, you will need to invest in specialist paints. Don't try to skimp on these — if you use

Once you start to stencil, you will find that you can easily adapt the different elements of border designs such as Stencil-Ease's® Floral Sculpture to create a charming overall result.

artists' acrylic oil paints or emulsion [latex] paints they tend to smudge and smear and may ruin all your hard work. Another alternative is to use stencil crayons. These look very effective when demonstrated, but I would not recommend them as I find them very tiring and time-consuming to use. The nature of stencil crayons also means that it is almost impossible to mix colours consistently. And although stencil crayons are fast-drying, the colours need time to set. Nor would I advocate aerosol spray paints. Unless you are a professional artist or decorator who has been taught how to use an airbrush, you will find it very difficult to control the application of paint. You will also find aerosols very expensive for stencil work and prone to running. And, of course, they are a hazard to the environment and can give off toxic fumes. Specialist, fast-drying stencil paints were originally formulated in the USA. After extensive research, I found these to be by far the most reliable paints for stencilling. This led me to pioneer the introduction of my own, fast-drying stencil paints. I consider stencil paints to be a vital part of any stenciller's equipment as they dry very quickly, minimize the risk of smearing and give instant professional shading. A little goes a long way; for most room projects, one pot for each colour will be sufficient, but allow two or more pots for border and floor projects in large rooms.

Carolyn Warrender's hard-surface stencil paints These fast-drying stencil paints have been developed as definitive colours in their own right. They are equally effective when mixed together, allowing you an infinite variety of colour possibilities.

FAST-DRYING STENCIL PAINTS

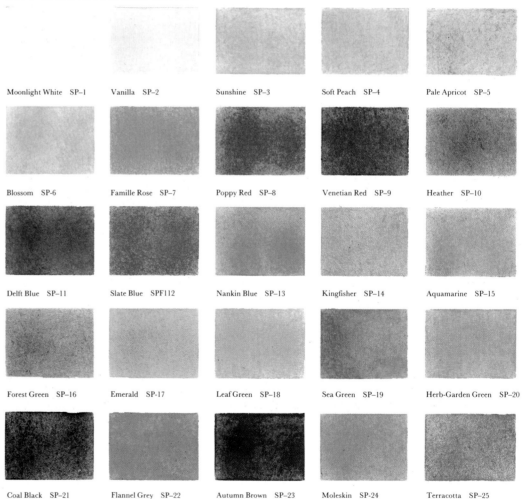

Moonlight White SP–1   Vanilla SP–2   Sunshine SP–3   Soft Peach SP–4   Pale Apricot SP–5

Blossom SP–6   Famille Rose SP–7   Poppy Red SP–8   Venetian Red SP–9   Heather SP–10

Delft Blue SP–11   Slate Blue SPF112   Nankin Blue SP–13   Kingfisher SP–14   Aquamarine SP–15

Forest Green SP–16   Emerald SP–17   Leaf Green SP–18   Sea Green SP–19   Herb-Garden Green SP–20

Coal Black SP–21   Flannel Grey SP–22   Autumn Brown SP–23   Moleskin SP–24   Terracotta SP–25

Fab-Tex® fabric paints

These fabric paints have been specially formulated by Stencil-Ease® to give wonderful translucent shading. Like hard-surface paints, they are fast drying, intermixable and, unlike many textile paints, do not leave a skin on the fabric.

FABRIC PAINTS

White FP–S17	Golden Yellow FP–S21	Savannah Peach FP–S28	Petal Pink FP–S32	Bright Red FP–S11
Concorde Blue FP–S25	Primary Blue FP–S20	Country Blue FP–S05	English Lavender FP–S29	Cranberry FP–S18
Navy Blue FP–S24	Telemark Green FP–S08	Dark Green FP–S13	Salem Green FP–S06	Mint Green FP–S22
Black FP–S16	Historic Brown FP–S10	Barn Red FP–S02		

We make a selection of china hog brushes developed in sizes for all stencilling projects. The size of brush you buy will depend on the size of the stencil you are using. With stencils of two or more colours, it is best to use a larger brush for the main colour and smaller brush sizes for the secondary details, unless there is no marked difference in scale between the different colours on your design. Mini-brushes are invaluable for fine details such as small petals, leaf shading and architectural stencils. For the best results, use a separate brush for each colour.

Hard-surface brushes

– HSB–2   For small designs. Architextures and secondary colours.
– HSB–4   Medium size. Most useful for general use.
– HSB–6   For floors and large designs.

These brushes can also be used for fabrics, although use of the fabric brushes is recommended.

Multi-purpose mini-brushes

– MSB–2   Smallest size for tiny details.
– MSB–4   For shading and Architextures.

Fabric brushes

– FSB–8   For general fabrics stencilling.
– FSB–12   For use on large designs when fabric stencilling.

STENCILLING CHECKLIST

As well as stencils, paints and brushes, you will also need the following items before you start your project. You will probably find that you already have most of them in your home; what you don't have you will be able to purchase from any hardware merchant, DIY shop or home decorating store.

YOU WILL NEED

Paper towel	Masking tape
Washing up liquid	Pencil
White spirit [mineral spirits]	Ruler
Scrap paper	Eraser
A large foil or plastic freezer container	Elastic bands
	Tracing paper
A small foil or plastic freezer container	Steel measuring rule
	Old jam jars
Lollipop sticks (for mixing your paints)	Stepladder
A plumb line (only necessary if you are stencilling a vertical design)	Apron or other protective clothing
	Scissors

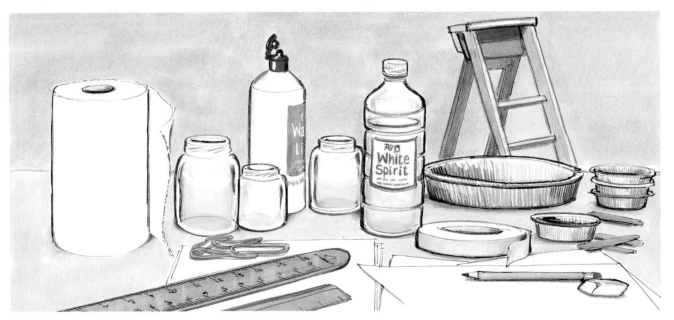

Planning and Measuring Up

Whatever your project, you must plan and measure before you start. You can follow these basic principles for all forms of stencilling:

BORDER DESIGNS

Start by measuring the length of the surface to be decorated and mark the centre point lightly with a pencil. Calculate how many times you will need to repeat the stencil to reach each corner. Always lengthen a design if it does not end exactly at the corner of a wall — if you are using a floral border, add a few extra petals rather than leaving a conspicuous gap. Lengthening a design is always preferable to half-finishing an additional design because an extended design will, through an optical illusion, appear to the observer to be balanced, whilst a shortened one will stand out and unbalance the overall design.

Stencil the dominant wall first, then move to the one opposite and last to your left and right. This will ensure a balanced result.

INDIVIDUAL MOTIFS

Use a ruler to work out approximate positions and mark their centre points in pencil to ensure even spacing. For a symmetrical design, follow the instructions given in these illustrated diagrams.

LARGER PROJECTS

These are best planned by practising trial runs on pieces of scrap paper. Experiment with different intensities of the colours you have chosen and pin them up on to the surface you plan to stencil. Hold these paper proofs against other objects that will be in the same room to see whether the colours sing or shout at each other. The proofs can also be useful when measuring up your wallspace. If you feel undecided, leave the scrap paper pinned

All-over designs giving the effect of a patterned wallpaper need to be measured up on a grid pencilled directly onto the surface. Take care that the scale of your design matches the scale of the grid.

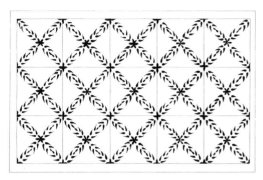

This design uses every square in the grid.

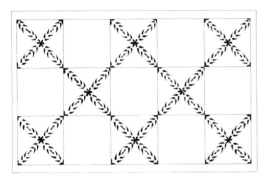

This design uses alternate squares in the grid.

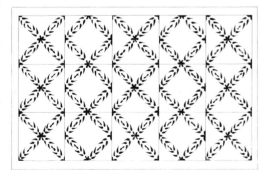

This design is centred on the cross-points of the vertical and horizontal lines.

INCORRECT

This design has been stencilled from one corner to the other. The result is asymetrical.

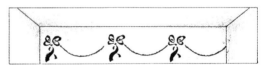

CORRECT

This design has been stencilled working outwards in each direction from the centre, to create a balanced result.

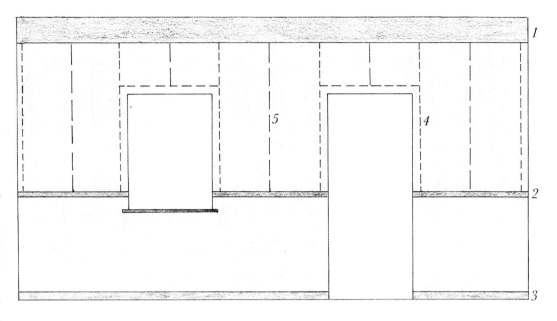

RIGHT: *For elaborate wall stencilling, measure up the area and stencil your design in the following sequence:*
1. *Ceiling border/picture rail*
2. *Dado rail*
3. *Skirting board*
4. *Borders around doors and windows*
5. *Vertical designs*

up for a day or two — you may find that after looking at it for a while you realise that a small adjustment in scale, colour or position makes a pleasing difference. Remember too that colours change under artificial light. Do believe in your own instincts and resist the temptation to rush about asking the advice of everyone you know — they will all have different views and you will be wretched if you forego your own scheme for the sake of someone else's bright idea only to find that you dislike the outcome. However, don't be recklessly impetuous. It is far better to live with a design for a few days and work out ways of improving it than to plunge in and then feel dissatisfied with the result.

RIGHT: *The sequence to follow when stencilling a border around a room. Always find the centre of the wall and stencil from the centre in both directions.*

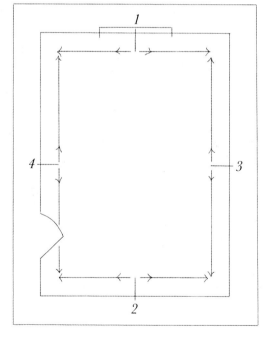

CREATING PANELS

Panelling a room is a long-established method of adding elegance and proportion to a space. In today's interiors, when so few of us have real wooden panelling, a similar effect can be achieved by painting and stencilling *trompe l'oeil* panels onto a plain, papered or painted wall. The smaller the room, the more dramatic the effect!

Start by looking at the room, taking note of all its focal points, such as windows, fireplaces and main pieces of furniture. Does the room have a cornice, skirting board or picture rail? Do you want to make the space look larger or smaller?

Once you have a few basic ideas in

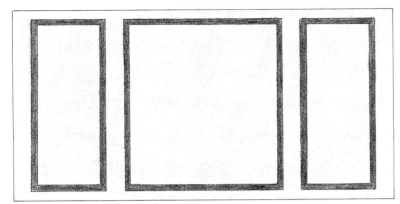

A few large panels make small rooms seem larger.

A narrow window can be given better proportions by adding single panels on either side.

Fireplaces look very effective with a panel on either side and one above.

Windows can also be widened by adding part panels on either side.

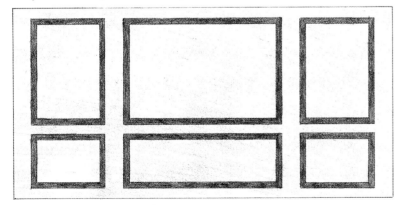

Panels used in pairs create a dado effect. Make sure that the break is at dado height (approximately 34 in/86 cm above floor level).

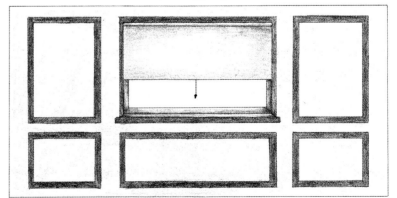

A panel used under a window with a blind blends in well when using panels in pairs.

mind, sketch all four sides of the room on a piece of paper, marking all of the focal points. Use our diagrams on the previous page to decide what sizes of panel would look best, making sure that they are in proportion to everything else in the room. Then draw the plan to scale on graph paper, working out the exact proportions of each panel.

Now, taking a plumb line or long ruler and pencil, measure your wall space, marking in all of the measurements. A pencil line must be drawn over plumb lines before starting to stencil. In most cases, the pencil line will be covered by paint once you start to stencil, but if you want to rub out the pencil line, leave the stencilling for twenty-four hours before you do so.

Choose a narrow stencil border design to co-ordinate with other furnishings in your room. Our Easy Peasy, Stencil-Ease's® Hearts & Flowers Border and Strawberry Border are some that create effective panels.

NOTE: Horizontal lines should be ½-1 in (1-2 cm) wider than vertical lines, depending on the size of the room as horizontal designs always look narrower than vertical ones.

VERTICAL PATTERNS

If you have planned a large floor or wall stencil design which includes vertical patterns, the best way to mark accurate vertical lines to follow is by using a plumb line and chalk box. To do this, you will need an assistant. Suspend the plumb line from the highest point of the wall that the stencil will cover and let the chalk box drop gently downwards, so that it dangles free of the floor. When the line is steady, ask your assistant to hold it firmly against the wall, then 'pluck' the line so that it leaves a straight chalk mark against the surface. You can remove the chalk later with a clean rag or eraser.

STRIPES

To stencil stripes of any width, you will need some sheets of plastic, which can be obtained through our shop and specialist stores. Alternatively, for narrow stripes on strong surfaces, you can use masking tape, as illustrated. First, draw a guide line in pencil on the surface you intend to stencil. If you are stencilling the full length of a wall or floor, mark this by using a plumb line as described above for vertical patterns. Then cut the plastic into two strips and position them on the surface with the machine-cut edges acting as the outer borders of the stripe. Secure the plastic strips with masking tape along the outer, hand-cut edges. Stencil in the space between the strips, stopping a little short of the end of the plastic so that when you reposition the strips there is a slight overlap to help you align the next section of the stripe. Do not let the paint overlap. Once you have completed your stripes they can be left plain or have another design stencilled over them.

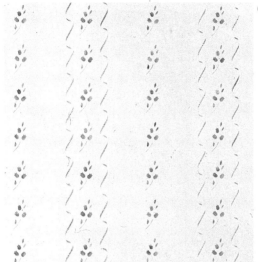

You can use stencil borders to create vertical stripes. Here, the use of the central motif only for every other stripe creates additional interest and avoids monotony.

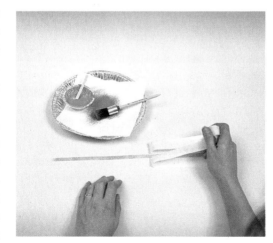

Peeling away the masking tape from a stencilled stripe.

STENCILLING STEP-BY-STEP

Assemble all the materials you need, and read the instructions on your paint pots and stencils before you begin. Check your measurements to make sure that they are correct.

CORRECT PAINT SHADING

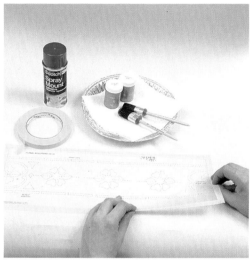

1. Position the stencil on the surface to be decorated and secure all the outer edges with masking tape. Spray adhesive is an alternative method of fixing the stencil and is advisable for detailed designs and delicate surfaces.

Remove loose pieces of the stencil before use. Use a sharp knife if necessary and never tear the stencil.

2. Stir the paint with a lollipop stick. Dip the very tip of your brush into a small amount poured into a small foil container. Then work almost all of the paint off the brush onto a dry paper towel folded in a larger foil container. Practise on scrap paper until no blotches appear and the brush is virtually dry.

3. Holding the brush like a pencil in one hand, and giving extra support to the stencil with the other hand, start stencilling. Pressing very lightly, move the brush clockwise and anti-clockwise with a circular motion. Start at the outer edges and slowly move inwards. In this way, you will be able to control your application of colour and build it up gradually to create the shades and colour tones you require.

PAINT TOO WET   PAINT TOO DRY

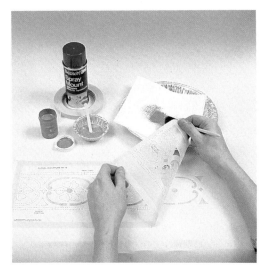  

4. Gently peel off the masking tape and lift up the stencil to check your progress. Don't worry if you make a few mistakes to begin with; you will soon learn how to avoid them!

5. Reposition your stencil using the printed register marks on the template. For single-colour stencils, simply repeat until the required area has been stencilled. For stencils of two or more colours, complete one colour and allow time for this to dry before applying the second colour.

6. To apply a second colour, position your template over the first colour, using the printed design lines as a guide. Prepare your brush for stencilling in the new colour and proceed as before.

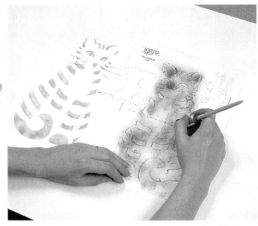

Mirror images of the same design can easily be stencilled by reversing the stencil:

1. *Apply the first design, using the stencil face up*
2. *Take care to clean off any remaining paint*
3. *Dry the stencil thoroughly*
4. *Repeat the design, using the reverse side of the stencil*

FABRIC STENCILLING

The best fabrics for stencilling are plain cottons. Avoid synthetic fibres, wool and textured cloths. Pre-wash your fabric and when it is dry iron out any creases. Pin the fabric to a smooth, flat surface to prevent movement while stencilling and follow the stage-by-stage instructions as illustrated, using Stencil-Ease's® Fab-Tex paints. Leave the completed work overnight, then 'fix' the design with an iron set at the temperature appropriate to the fabric you are using — don't use steam. Do a trial run on a small patch of the fabric to check that the heat of the iron does not lift the paint. Then heat-set the stencil by ironing back and forth across the cloth, letting the iron rest for twenty-five to thirty seconds on the stencilled areas. Large items can be heat-set in commercial launderette dryers. Set the dryer for a forty-five-minute programme at a high temperature.

Stencilled fabrics should be hand-washed gently in cool, soapy water or machine-washed using a programme for delicate fabrics. Dry cleaning is not recommended.

Stencilling on fabric can be particularly effective when used instead of more traditional techniques such as tapestry.

You can create an extravagant look from plain curtain fabric by stencilling it, as Colleen Bery has here, to complement your other furnishings.

Professional shaded results can be achieved on fabrics and hard surfaces by stencilling one or more additional colours over the initial stencil colour.

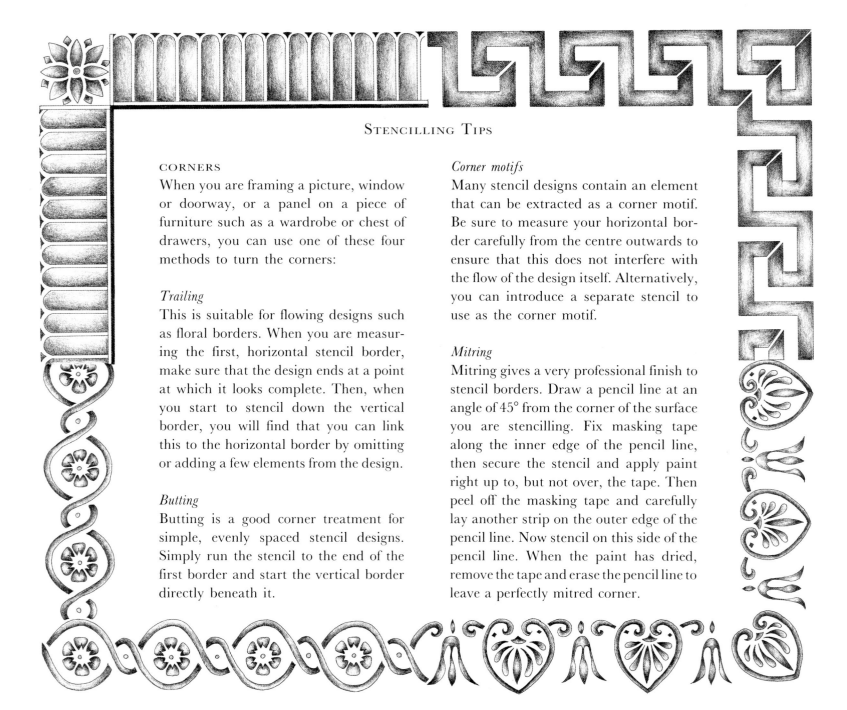

STENCILLING TIPS

CORNERS

When you are framing a picture, window or doorway, or a panel on a piece of furniture such as a wardrobe or chest of drawers, you can use one of these four methods to turn the corners:

Trailing

This is suitable for flowing designs such as floral borders. When you are measuring the first, horizontal stencil border, make sure that the design ends at a point at which it looks complete. Then, when you start to stencil down the vertical border, you will find that you can link this to the horizontal border by omitting or adding a few elements from the design.

Butting

Butting is a good corner treatment for simple, evenly spaced stencil designs. Simply run the stencil to the end of the first border and start the vertical border directly beneath it.

Corner motifs

Many stencil designs contain an element that can be extracted as a corner motif. Be sure to measure your horizontal border carefully from the centre outwards to ensure that this does not interfere with the flow of the design itself. Alternatively, you can introduce a separate stencil to use as the corner motif.

Mitring

Mitring gives a very professional finish to stencil borders. Draw a pencil line at an angle of 45° from the corner of the surface you are stencilling. Fix masking tape along the inner edge of the pencil line, then secure the stencil and apply paint right up to, but not over, the tape. Then peel off the masking tape and carefully lay another strip on the outer edge of the pencil line. Now stencil on this side of the pencil line. When the paint has dried, remove the tape and erase the pencil line to leave a perfectly mitred corner.

FIXING STENCILS

When you are fixing and removing stencils, be careful not to damage the background surface. If you are stencilling onto a fragile surface, it is safer to use drawing pins or spray adhesive than masking tape to hold the stencil in place.

WORKING WITH A STEPLADDER

If you need a stepladder for a high border design, never *never never* leave your stencil paints and brushes at the top of the ladder. This chapter could be filled with cautionary stories of professional decorators who have overlooked this rule and ruined their work by inadvertently bumping into the ladder and splattering paint in every direction.

AWKWARD BENDS

Plastic stencils are themselves flexible and by working with them you will find you are able to manoeuvre your way round bends in walls and pieces of furniture without too much difficulty, but it is wise to give the stencil added support with your hand to be certain that the design does not slip.

HAND PAINTED DETAILS

Use a small artist's brush to add final details to your design, such as an animal's eye or the veins of a leaf.

VARNISHING

Varnishing is only necessary when the surfaces you have stencilled are to be in constant use and so need protection from wear and tear. This applies mainly to floors, floorcloths and furniture.

Wait at least four days after stencilling and test a small area first. This may seem like an unnecessarily long time, given the fast-drying nature of stencil paints, but it is vital because there tends to be a chemical interaction between the ingredients of the paint and the varnish and the paint needs to be absolutely bone dry to prevent this interaction. Use a clear polyeurethane varnish, following the manufacturer's instructions. Bear in mind that the colour of your stencils is likely to darken and yellow slightly when varnish is applied.

MENDING A TORN STENCIL

If you take good care of them, your stencils will last for many years. If you do tear one, however, it can easily be repaired by sticking sellotape or masking tape on both sides and recutting the design.

AFTERCARE

YOURSELF

Unless you are a window cleaner, a professional decorator or a keep-fit enthusiast, you may be fairly stiff after a major stencilling session. Don't try to stencil for more than five hours at a time. When you've finished, treat yourself to a long shower or a leisurely wallow in the bath. And when you've completed your project, why not treat those muscles you never knew you had to a sauna or massage?

YOUR STENCILS

After each session, clean your stencils gently on both sides with a paper towel dampened in warm, soapy water. Stains and spray adhesive can be removed with white spirit [mineral spirits].

When they have been cleaned and dried, put your stencils back in their original packaging and store them flat under heavy books, trunks or wine cases, in a place where you won't forget them!

BRUSHES

Always wash your brushes well in warm, soapy water, then rinse them clean. Wrap an elastic band around the bristles so that they hold their shape and leave them to dry overnight. Never stencil with a wet brush. A useful tip to revive neglected brushes is to wash them in white spirit, rinse in soapy water and apply a small amount of hair conditioner. Rinse off, and the brushes should be as transformed as tired hair!

PAINTS

Paint pots should be stored in a cool, dry place. Wipe any excess paint off the pot and the lid using white spirit. Close each pot tightly. Paints mixed to your own colours can be stored in airtight jam jars.

PART II

INTERIORS

ONE

HALLS, STAIRWAYS, CORRIDORS

If you were invited to have one room in your newly transformed house decorated from top to toe, which one would you choose? As likely as not, you would opt for a reception room or bedroom, a place where you could look forward to relaxing for hours at a stretch and lapping up your newly transformed surroundings. Many of us, when we buy a new house or give our current accommodation a facelift, put halls, corridors and stairways low on our list of priorities. They need to look presentable, of course, but we naturally tend to spend more thought, effort and money on the rooms in which we spend most of our time. All too often, halls, corridors and stairways stand neglected, while the rooms to which they lead are lovingly stripped, painted, glazed and stencilled into shape as they prepare to play the starring roles in our homes. This is particularly true of small townhouses,

where the hall space often seems at first glance to be too insignificant to be worth lavishing very much time and attention on. In larger properties and country houses, where the hall is large enough to be treated as a reception room as well as a thoroughfare, the decorating potential is more obvious, the challenge more direct. But those narrow entrance halls, steep staircases and dark passageways that characterize so many town houses and city apartments have their role to perform as well. They take pride of place at the start of this section not only because they are the first areas of the home that greet you when you open the front door, but also because they play a vital role in drawing together the different rooms and levels of the home, and creating an environment which is a harmonious whole, rather than a discordant jumble of unrelated styles.

HALLS

As you knock on the front door of a house you haven't visited before, do you feel your curiosity quicken as you wait for the door to open and reveal what lies beyond? And do you feel a twinge of disappointment if it then opens into a characterless, colourless entrance hall? First impressions count, however fleeting they may be! So if you want the first impression your guests receive of your home to be a favourable one, and if you want your spirits to be lifted when you turn the key in the door every evening, you can't afford to ignore your hallway. Remember too that this more than any

In this country hallway, stencilled borders are used to frame the whole of each wall in colours that echo those of the richly patterned carpet.

other room gives the clearest indication of a house's style and period. Whether your hall is the size of a shoebox or an aeroplane hangar, your stencil kit will be a faithful ally if you want to do justice to this area, which is the first indication to visitors of your taste, your style and the character of your home.

Even the narrowest hall or entrance passage has advantages that other rooms don't possess. The two most obvious of these advantages may seem on the surface to be drawbacks in decorative terms. First, many halls act primarily as thoroughfares, not as living areas in their own right. But, as such, they are ideal settings for more daring and dramatic effects than you might choose in a part of the house that enjoys more regular use. Secondly, halls of this type do not have an obvious focal point such as a fireplace or an important piece of furniture. Well and good! For this means that there will be nothing to distract the eye from the impact of your stencils, and the less furniture you can accommodate in your hall, the more uninterrupted wall space you have to play with.

These two factors combine to make halls the ideal location for large-scale stencil murals and *trompe l'oeil* effects. If you choose to buy pre-cut stencils, you will have a considerable range of designs to choose from:

— For subtle, subdued architectural *trompe l'oeil*, take your pick from my Architextures collection: Greek Key for a clean, clear, classical effect in a single colourway; Arcadia or Daisy Chain, with their balance of simple curves and straight, narrow borders for a softer, more lyrical result; the exuberant lines of Utopia for a hallway that is guaranteed to lift your spirits whenever you wander through it.
— For a more informal atmosphere, try one of Adele Bishop's floral designs such as Southern Impressions, Hancock Border, Southfield or Grand Garland. Or continue the tradition of the Southern States of the USA, where pineapples symbolize hospitality; choose between Pineapple Frieze and Colonial Pineapple – or use both!
— If you live in the country, or want to spirit a little rural atmosphere into your city surroundings, you can create lovely results with designs such as Stencil-Ease's® Hancock Oak Leaf, Willow Tree or — one of the prettiest stencils of them all — Rose Peony Urn.

Bright blue paint creates a dramatic background for the tiny stencilled hallway of this London apartment, created by Francis and Sarah Roos.

TOP LEFT: Trompe l'oeil *trellis work and pillars give a stylish decorative finish to this tiled hall. The carefully shaded grey of the stencils complements the dark furniture, and the two facing mirrors increase the sense of openness and space.*

NEAR LEFT: *A touch of drama in passing from one room to the next: a daring carmine cornice and ribbon-and-bow stencils pick up the themes in the fabric of the* portière.

BOTTOM LEFT: *An otherwise unremarkable wall space on a half landing can become an important decorative feature when stencilled. This pretty border and bouquet design also emphasizes the fresh, spring colours of the curtains in the window recess.*

Whatever atmosphere you want to create, remember that you can combine elaborate motifs with simple borders, and that if you want a bold effect you need to choose colours that contrast with the background wall colour. They should also harmonize with the colour of your flooring, and with the colours of the rooms that lead directly off the hall — but don't let these precautions stop you from being adventurous!

STAIRWAYS

Many stairways lead directly off entrance halls and, like these, they enjoy the advantages of plenty of unrestricted wall space. In fact, you may feel there is too much wall! If you live in a three- or four-storey townhouse, you may find yourself wondering how high you should run your design — and how high you and your stepladder can reach! One way of resolving this is to contain your design within a framework that rises just above eye level, and ignore the wall space above. Take your cue from the measurements you work to at ground level and repeat these as your design climbs the staircase. If you wish, you can carry the same design throughout the house. But if you have several flights of stairs, which

Stencilled flowerpots add a witty touch to a simple wooden staircase.

are broken by landings, you may wish to change tack, using a fairly formal border up to the first floor landing, and a simpler, more naive design for a higher flight of stairs leading to less sophisticated children's rooms or spare bedrooms.

Is your staircase carpeted to your satisfaction? If it is, then you will not need to use stencils on the steps themselves, though a stencilled floorcloth will give extra character to your landing areas. If you do have uncarpeted stairs and you want to create a clean, neo-colonial atmosphere in your home, using stencils on the vertical part of each step will not only add visual interest but also demarcate each tread more clearly — particularly useful on steep back stairs. Be sure, though, to varnish these stencils with polyeurethane as protection against scuffing.

CORRIDORS

Corridors. What is to be done about them? Long, narrow, often poorly lit, they can test the imagination of the most experienced designer. And they conjure up dismal memories of draughty school passages, unloved offices, inept conversions.

But even the dreariest corridor can be turned into one of character and charm. Indeed, the longer the corridor, the more potential there can be. If you live in an apartment that is on one level, you can break the monotony of the passageway by scooping a swathe of fabric across it to separate the reception area from the bathrooms and bedrooms, or build in an extra door to divide the space and retain more heat in winter. As often as not, you will find that your corridors offer space for storage, either for narrow bookcases or for fitted cupboards or wardrobes. And if you have a corridor that rounds a corner, this is the ideal space to be ingenious with a wall mirror or a *trompe l'oeil* mural.

Where do stencils fit into all this? As we discussed in Part I, a series of stencilled panels will open out a narrow passage and create the illusion of more space (see page 46). So too will a combination of designs that creates a contrast between the area from skirting board to dado, and that from dado to ceiling. Even if you do no more than frame your doorways and windows with a simple, stencilled border, linking them to each other with a continuation of the same border, you will redeem this part of your home and turn your corridors into areas which are not to be hurried through like subway passages, but are a positive pleasure to look at and to live with.

BELOW LEFT: *Oriental* trompe l'oeil *stencils in the classic combination of blue on yellow make this an irresistibly pretty corridor and take away the need for pictures.*
BELOW: *How to give proportion to a narrow stairway: Stencil Ease's® Newport Trellis runs up this split-level stairway at dado height and also borders the doors and windows.*

THE HALL AND STAIRS OF OUR LONDON HOME

Many nineteenth-century townhouses have frustratingly narrow entrance halls, and ours is no exception. What could we do with this space? We wanted a decorative scheme that would make a dramatic impact. We also wanted to use colours that would link this area to the rest of the house. Of course, this meant that before we started work we had more or less to decide on a decorative plan that could be extended to all the other rooms, and it didn't take us long to settle upon the discipline of a co-ordinating grey and moleskin architectural colour scheme. This is the only staircase in a three-storey house of modest proportions, and we did not feel this gave us sufficient space to be able to alter the design on any floor without reducing the sense of space. On the contrary, our intention here and else-where was to integrate stencilling into an overall decorative plan that would create an atmosphere as light, spacious and sophisticated as the scale of the house would allow.

Stencilling at its most sophisticated: the Egg and Dart design from the Architextures collection combines with marblizing and ragging to create a stunning trompe l'oeil *panel.*

We started by putting a dado rail round the entrance hall and up each flight of stairs to the top of the house. Although this involved a little extra time and expense before we could start decorating and stencilling, in the long run it had three advantages: first, the dado rail imposed a sense of architectural order; secondly, its inclusion meant that we had less space to wallpaper so we were able to spend less on wallpaper than we would have had to if we had papered from skirting board to ceiling; thirdly, it is better able to withstand the onslaught of suitcases, shopping and vacuum cleaners than wallpaper. We chose a grey and white striped wallpaper from Zoffany because the narrow, vertical lines emphasize the height of the walls and also because the design and colours make a suitable background for black-and-white prints, line drawings and muted watercolours.

We then glazed and marblized the area below the dado and used the Egg and Dart stencil from my Architextures collection to create a panelled effect. Because we were stencilling onto a glazed surface, we held the stencil in place with very sparing amounts of spray adhesive, rather than masking tape, so as not to damage the glaze. It was important with this project to use a stencil that did not create problems at corners and you can see that we in fact mitred the corner of each panel. The paints we used for this stencil were a mixture of Flannel Grey and Moleskin with just a whisper of Coal Black.

We continued the architectural effect of the stencilled panels through to the woodwork, glazing and dragging all of the skirting boards, cupboards and doorways in the hall and on the upper landings.

This very sophisticated use of stencilling in a *trompe l'oeil* design scheme gives the hall and staircase a distinctively classical character and no one believes that the panels have been stencilled until we explain exactly how we realized the design. The whole decoration took several weeks to execute, as each stage of paintwork had to be left to dry and the area to be covered was quite considerable, and the stencilling itself took ten days, working panel by panel every evening.

TOP: *The view up the first flight of stairs.*
BOTTOM: *Looking down from the top landing to the door onto our roof terrace.*

'IN MARBLE HALLS . . .'

'I can't resist going into churches!' It was the marble at Brompton Oratory, London, that gave Marika Brennan the inspiration for the hall and staircase of her home, although of course the original is not *trompe l'oeil* but genuine marble, nor is it stencilled. Nevertheless, Marika has adapted the design at the oratory in a way which corresponds perfectly to a small-scale domestic setting.

Marika papered the space between dado and ceiling with a simple yellow-and-white stripe and concentrated her painting skills on the lower part of the walls. She divided the area into panels that were framed with a yellow glaze, lightly marblized and each containing a grey disc. This design runs right round the hall and up to the top of the stairs. Marika then used the Easy Peasy stencil from the Architextures collection as a grey border detail on the glaze, adapting the stencil to cope with the curved edges of the central discs. By using *trompe l'oeil* in this way, she has succeeded in making the narrow staircase seem much wider than it really is.

Easy Peasy stencils border the central panels of this trompe l'oeil *dado design.*

The staircase opens onto a small, rectangular landing which has been painted plain white. Here, an ornate, engraved glass lantern with its gilded leaves formed the basis for a decorative plan based on Stencil-Ease's® Thompson House Frieze. The lantern is one of Marika's many bargain purchases and was picked up for next to nothing in a London junk shop. The stencil design is of dancing leaves and these give what could otherwise be a rather dark, poorly lit area a deceptively open-air character. With its disciplined borders, the frieze also emphasizes the architectural features on the landing.

This leafy stencil also complements the decorations of two of the bedrooms leading off the landing, where leaf patterns are again the dominant theme. The colours used for the project were Autumn Brown and Forest Green.

ABOVE: *A complete change of character greets you on the upper landing, which has been stencilled with Thompson House Frieze.*
LEFT: *The panelled theme has been modified for the angles of the staircase.*

A COTSWOLD FARMHOUSE

These simple yet strikingly effective stencilled hallways form part of an eighteenth-century Cotswold farmhouse with sixteenth-century origins. Both schemes were designed by David Mendel for Francis Burne. The simpler leaf stencil is in the entrance hall, and a more elaborate design, again with leaf motifs, has been adopted on an upper corridor. Throughout, the interior of the house has been beautifully decorated with a variety of techniques, including glazed paint finishes, flat paint, *trompe l'oeil*, wallpaper and stencils, since Francis Burne believes that, when used with discretion, different treatments can complement individual rooms without competing against each other, and that together they contribute to a distinctive and visually unified interior.

Much of the entrance hall as it now stands is in fact a recent addition to the house, having been added in the last decade. In order for the walls to be in keeping with the character of the period, it was important to get their texture right, so they have been plastered and

The rough plasterwork of the entrance hall needs only the simplest stencil motifs to emphasize its charm.

TOP: *Detail of the hall stencil. Note how the colours alternate throughout the design.*

RIGHT: *Upstairs, a more elaborate leaf motif runs around the top of the walls and frames a doorway and window.*

BOTTOM: *The veins of each leaf have been carefully hand-painted after stencilling.*

then left with a rough finish. Stencilling was chosen as being the form of decoration that would best enhance this wall treatment while being true to the age of the room. Like the wall surfaces, the stencils have been applied with subdued, natural colours that relate well to the rural surroundings of the farmhouse.

In the upper corridor, the leaf theme is repeated but this time in a more elaborate, though monotone, border design. In each of the two stencilled areas, which are at opposite ends of the corridor, it is interesting to note how the window and door, although using in principle the same design, each becomes an original and pleasing focal point with a character of its own. Small but significant finishing touches, such as the hand-painted veining of each leaf and the decision to let the central leaf in the frame above the door break over the border, make this a highly professional example of custom stencilling.

On the border above the window, a discreet flourish is introduced where the central leaf breaks the discipline of the rest of the design.

TWO

SITTING ROOMS AND STUDIES

In most homes, the sitting room is the main reception room and, as such, the most important reflection of its owner's taste. This is where you will do most of your entertaining, whether formal or informal. Your visitors are likely to see more of your sitting room than of any other room in the house. So if you take pride in the decoration of your home, you will want this part of it to be a real credit to you. Sitting rooms are also places for you and other members of your household to relax in, and one of the best ways to ensure that you will be able to unwind in this, as in any room, is to decorate it in a way which is inviting, attractive and comfortable. It's not surprising that when most people move house they concentrate their first efforts on making a sitting room in which everyone will feel at ease with themselves and their surroundings. Stencilling provides an infinitely versatile means of achieving this.

SITTING ROOMS

The way in which you stencil your sitting room will depend to some extent on its function, which in turn depends on the type and size of your home, and the number and ages of the people living there. Do you have enough space to make this a formal reception room and create another, more casual, family room somewhere else? If so, it is worth considering stencils that are grand in style and scale, such as Stencil-Ease's® Floral Sculpture or Winthrop Border, the Architextures collection or the Paintability range.

Do you have lively children who use the sitting room for playing games and watching television? In this case, you will create a more carefree atmosphere using stencils from the Folk Art collection designed by Stencil-Ease®. Do you dwell in solitary splendour in a city penthouse where the reception area is open-plan and you want a modern decor? Then think about using Adele Bishop's Japanese stencils, or a geometric design such as Free Spirit. Is this a room where you will flop into a sofa after a day's work and listen to jazz records? Is it a room where you will organize children's tea parties or late night bops? As likely as not, you will find yourself using it for more than one function, and spending more of your waking hours in it than anywhere else. So it's worth mulling a while over what you want and experimenting with various colour schemes before you roll up your sleeves and set yourself to work.

Unashamedly baroque stencil designs grace the walls of this magnificent apartment. Beyond the doorway, the trompe l'oeil *curtains and pilaster details have also been achieved with stencils.*

Stencilled borders and a framed bouquet of flowers make a charming central feature above the fireplace of this country sitting room.

FOCAL POINTS

When you have chosen the stencil you like best, bear in mind the focal point of the sitting room as you decide how to position your design. In old houses and apartments, this is often the fireplace. In the absence of this, it may be a window, or a coffee table which is placed in the centre of a group of chairs and sofas. Many large reception rooms have a fireplace on one wall, but need an additional focal point in another part of the room. If your sitting room is sparsely furnished and lacks interest, you would do well to use large stencil motifs to create colour and character on the walls. If on the other hand you want a design that does not compete against a lovely Georgian fireplace or fine pieces of furniture, select stencils and colours that will quietly complement these without overpowering them. If you have a lot of wall space that needs to be broken up, combine vertical and horizontal borders in a series of panels that contain complementary motifs — consider the possibilities of Bouquet & Borders or the Shelburne sets. But exercise restraint if you have a collection of pictures to hang on the walls.

SUMMER STENCILS, WINTER STENCILS

Whatever the size and role of your sitting room, one way to ensure that you will not tire of your decoration too quickly is to concentrate on stencilling your soft furnishings and drapes and having one set for summer and one for winter. This old-fashioned custom is one that disappeared with the advent of central heating, which did away with the need to have thick, heavy curtains and upholstery fabrics to keep out the winter cold and lighter, brighter ones to celebrate the months of spring and summer. In fact, if you choose your materials with a little care, you can return to this tradition without spending very much money at all.

To use stencils effectively in this way, you need to choose carpeting and wall paints that are pale and neutral, such as whites, creams, beiges or the softest pastels. Buy plain lampshades, and plain fabrics for cushions, floorcloths, curtains, table covers, blinds and upholstery fabrics. By selecting one set of fabrics, stencils and colours for winter and another for summer you will be able to capture the spirit of the different seasons in a style that is imaginative, economical

Studies

In contrast to sitting rooms, studies are often rooms which are idiosyncratic in character. Whatever their main role, be it as an office for an academic or simply a retreat for writing letters and watching television, studies are frequently decorated for their owner and no-one else. And so they should be! Why compromise if this is the one part of the house or flat where you can enjoy spending time by yourself and where you don't have to accommodate anyone else's possessions or create space for company other than when you choose to do so? If you are lucky enough to have a study which you can call your own, indulge yourself in its decoration. This is the one part of the home which is your own inalienable territory. Enjoy it! If you want to be outrageously feminine, then be so, with floral borders and individual motifs such as Stencil-Ease's® Tulip Basket, Whig Rose, Wreath of Flowers or Carnations. If you are a bachelor or harassed husband who wants this room at least to be

and infinitely adaptable. In many ways, decorating a sitting room is a more exacting task than any other interior project, for it requires a number of disparate items of furniture — chairs, television, side tables, desks, lights, sofas, storage units — to be positioned in a harmonious fashion against a background that pulls the room as a whole together and creates

an environment that is relaxing and comfortable. If you concentrate on using stencils for your soft furnishings, you are sure to achieve that harmony and you will be able to control the result by adding to it or subtracting as you wish, and to transform the room completely at the first bite of autumn frost, and the first kiss of spring.

thoroughly masculine in character, select Greek Key, Castille, Daisy Chain or Egg and Dart from our Architextures collection and use them in conjunction with rich, dark paint glazes. Or recapture your boyhood with the frieze which makes up Soldier's Corner: bright drums, trumpets and three tall soldiers standing smartly to attention. And if you incline towards family mottos, Latin inscriptions or even lines of your favourite poetry, all of these can be transferred to your walls using stencil alphabets.

ABOVE: *The addition of a classically inspired frieze gives a special finish to these study bookshelves.*
LEFT: *Islamic motifs, gilded paints and fiery reds make this a rich Aladdin's cave of a study. Design by Alex Davidson.*

A LONDON DRAWING ROOM

People think, blink and look twice when they are told that this drawing room has been stencilled. And indeed, to an eye that has not been trained to observe how an interior has been put together, the role of the stencil in this room is certainly not immediately apparent. Nor is the fact that the walls have been broken into *trompe l'oeil* panels by dragging; or that the colour scheme shifts from blue and green to blue and red in the part of the room that leads into the dining area beyond; or even that these are in fact two rooms rather than one, with the central wall knocked through to create a double reception room.

This is a main reception room and as such it is frequently used for entertaining. In fact, it makes a perfect room for evening use, as it has only one, north-facing bay window and benefits from little natural light during the day. A large part of the philosophy behind the scheme here was to use architectural colours and decorative techniques so subtly that they would be absorbed more on a subcon-

The dado rail of this sitting room was originally too high. It has been lowered by adding a second, narrower rail and stencilling the space between with Waverley.

scious than a conscious level. It is above all a room which is intended to inspire a sense of elegance and comfort and to encourage those who use it to relax, let their tensions be banished and their troubles depart.

How was this effect achieved? First, the walls were glazed with a pale mixture of blue/green/grey so as to create an architectural character in the room. My husband Francis mixed the glaze and he took his cue for the colours from a large French oil painting. He broke the walls into a series of panels which open up the limited proportions of the room — it measures approximately 36ft × 12ft (10.8 × 3.6 metres). This colour scheme also makes a sympathetic background for the collection of drawings and watercolours that adorn the walls.

There was already a dado rail here, but it had been positioned too high, and so threw out the proportions of the room. This was corrected by putting in a second dado moulding 4 in (10 cm) below the first and stencilling the gap in between. Although the result may suggest that this was an easy job, in fact it took several days to complete. This was because there was no means of securing the stencil firmly onto the curved edges of the dado

On each stretch of wall, the design has been carefully measured from the centre so as to create a balanced result.

rails themselves. So the stencil had to be lightly secured with spray adhesive and the rail carefully transformed, step by step.

A special characteristic of this stencil design is its use of negative colour. The stencil, which is Waverley from the Architextures collection, has been painted in Vanilla against the dove grey basecoat, with the result that this background grey acts rather like a shadow and so helps the stencil to appear more like an authentic moulding than a two-dimensional design. This was a deliberate decorative device to make the stencil as true as possible to the classical moulding which inspired its design.

Another feature of this stencil is that it draws the two parts of the room together. In this respect, it plays a particularly important role as we have introduced green and blue as the chief colour combination in one half of the room, and red and blue in the second half to prepare for the red dining room which lies beyond the French windows. If this had been done without treating the walls and dado in such a way as to draw the two halves together, the result would have been fragmented and bitty, looking more like two disparate rooms than a single, unified reception area.

So, although at first glance the stencil seems to play an insignificant part in this decorative scheme, in fact it is one of the chief factors that contribute to the room's

success. However, it was not an easy project and while the result has certainly made the effort worthwhile, it is not a task I would recommend to an inexperienced stenciller.

TOP: *The design breaks unobtrusively to accommodate radiator covers.*

BOTTOM: *Detail of the Waverley stencil.*

A PRIVATE UTOPIA

Vanessa de Lisle, Executive Fashion Editor of *Vogue*, decided to create completely contrasting atmospheres in the two ground-floor rooms of her London home. The large, south-facing kitchen, which is featured on page 138, is very much a day room, while this boldly decorated sitting room is used almost exclusively at night.

The fabrics here are strong, dark pinks and reds, all of them in classic patterns: an archetypally English rose chintz from Colefax and Fowler has been chosen for

Utopia, from the Architextures collection, has been stencilled above the picture rail of this sitting room, taking up the dominant pink colours in the sofas and curtains.

the curtains; an old kelim lies in front of the fireplace; and rich paisley and tartan patterns cover two of the sofas. This almost bewilderingly eclectic mixture is successful on several counts: first, the sheer power and depth of the colours disguise the fact that the main pieces of furniture are fairly ordinary; secondly, the room has a marvellous feeling of warmth and comfort, in welcome contrast to the grey skies that hang over London nine months of the year; and in the evening, the combination of subdued lighting and strong colours creates a mood that is recognizably English yet at the same time has a strong exotic element.

The walls have been sponged with a very pale apricot glaze that looks pink on long, light summer evenings but becomes yellow when lit artificially on the dark nights of autumn and winter. This colour forms an excellent, understated background not only for the fabrics but also for the richly gilded antique mirrors and the dark paintings which are in fact reproduction prints, from the museum shop at the Prado in Madrid, but which have been transformed by clever framing. Special paint effects have also been used on the wooden mantlepiece, which was painted pale grey then lightly marblized.

To make a feature of the space between picture rail and ceiling, Vanessa chose the Utopia stencil from the Architextures collection. This has been painted in Venetian Red shaded with Coal Black and so complements the dominant red theme of the room. The classic form of the stencil also echoes the classic designs of the fabrics and it is this deliberate decision to stick to such traditional, well-tested shapes and patterns that is one of the main secrets behind the overall success of the room. A final, feminine touch is added by the narrow-stemmed vase which is filled with lilies throughout the winter, and pink roses when summer comes.

TOP: *The design is continued behind the curtain rail of the French windows.*
BOTTOM: *Detail of the Utopia stencil.*

A NEO-COLONIAL STUDY

This room is on the first floor of a typical, terraced London house, and had been used simply as storage space by the previous occupants. It continued to perform this role for the first few months after the owners had moved in while they concentrated on decorating the main reception rooms downstairs. But the possibilities for this small room were often discussed.

My brief was to decorate the room so that it could serve initially as a restful study, but it also had to be adaptable for use as a child's nursery at a later date. After turning over several approaches, I eventually decided that, small and insignificant though it may appear, this room could be given a distinctive neo-Colonial character. At the outset, the room was really very dull, with unimpressive proportions — 12ft × 15ft (3.6 × 4.5 metres) — no fireplace, no cornice and cheap bookshelves. My starting point was the one, south-facing, window, for which I

The yellow and grey Bernard Thorp curtain fabric sets the colour theme for this south-facing study. On the walls are Laurel Swag, Cordelia Border, Cordelia Tassel and English Bow. The floor stencil is an early Adele Bishop design, now discontinued.

designed yellow and grey patterned curtains. This combination then dictated the colour scheme for the rest of the room. The walls were covered with 'ragged' pale yellow wallpaper from Osborne and Little, and I disguised the cheap wood of the bookshelves with patterned, grey and white paper borders from Colefax and Fowler – a very fiddly job!

For me, stencilling a floor is one of the most wonderful ways of transforming a room. If I could, I would stencil all the floors in houses I decorate, but in this instance, this room was the only one in which the floorboards were of good enough quality to bear exposure. Another important influence on my decision was that the floor could be stencilled far more economically than it could be carpeted. Last but not least, if the room was to become a nursery, a stencilled floor would be easier to clean and protect from stains than a fitted carpet.

I chose an Adele Bishop floor stencil and agonized over what colours to adopt. For a while, everyone favoured the idea of a deep, rich red background colour, intending to create a kelim-like effect. Finally, it was decided that the best way to maximize the limited space of the room was to follow the muted grey of the curtains. The sanded surface was painted with three coats of bluish-white oil-based glaze, lightly applied so as to allow the grain of the wood to show through. Then two of us worked together on the stencil itself, which took the best part of a day to complete. For an amateur, approximately twice that time would have been needed — but anyone who takes up stencilling soon finds that the more you do, the faster you can work.

The handsome collection of classical prints that hang on the walls were found by the owner in Portobello Road. Their mounts have been lightly sponged with a grey/blue watercolour wash to draw them into the decorative scheme of the whole room. Arranged as they are, they also emphasize the room's height, which saves it from being a characterless box. However, the effect is controlled and contained by the addition of a stencilled cornice, Laurel Swag, while the Cordelia Border and Cordelia Tassel link the prints with the mirrors and plates that hang on the other walls and so give the room definition and unity.

TOP: *A handsome collection of prints hangs on the wall opposite the fireplace.*
MIDDLE: *Detail of an overall drawing decorated with Cordelia Swag and Cordelia Tassel.*
BOTTOM: *Detail of the floor stencil.*

THREE

DINING ROOMS

WHAT a luxury it is to have a house with a dining room! Over the last fifty years, we have become accustomed to informal open-plan living in homes where space is often at such a premium that sitting room and dining area have to be combined into a single living room. Alternatively, the kitchen doubles as a dining room, serving a dual function as the room where meals are both prepared and served. But nothing can compare with the attractions of a formal dining room. Nothing can whet the appetite more than the sight of a beautifully laid table, each carefully arranged place setting waiting for the guest to take his or her seat; sunshine or candlelight catching the edge of glasses, plates, cutlery, table napkins crisp and clean and neatly folded; chairs standing to attention until the moment when the food that is being prepared in the kitchen is ready, the guests are called to the table and the meal is served.

The role of the dining room in any house is obvious: it should be a place where flatmates, friends and family can relax and unwind as they eat; a place where conversation can flourish; a place where everyone feels able to enjoy themselves. For this to be realized, a primary consideration must be the comfort of the diners: the table should be big enough to accommodate everyone without each person jabbing his elbow into the person beside him; the chairs must be well made and comfortable; the light at evening meals should be neither clinically bright nor so dark that nobody can see what they're eating. Ask yourself which are your favourite restaurants and why you frequent them. Your reasons probably include your enjoyment of the ambiance as well as the standard of food and service. Next time you are in a restaurant, let yourself ponder on how this ambiance has been created. You will

perhaps be surprised when you start to notice how many restaurant owners use stencils as an effective yet inexpensive way of decorating their walls.

As with restaurants, one of the most daunting aspects of planning a dining room is the expense of the furniture — a dining room table and a set of six or eight chairs from even the cheapest store amounts to a considerable amount of money by many people's standards and, for most of us, the table and chairs we buy will be expected to do a long innings. They are certainly the crowning glory of any dining room and if they look wrong, the whole room looks wrong. Nothing looks more ridiculous than exquisitely decorated walls, splendid curtains and,

The panels of this stunning dining room have been ingeniously stencilled so as to look like marquetry.

in the middle of the room, a scuffed, shabby table and an ill-matched collection of tacky chairs. So the designer of any dining room needs to think first and foremost of these furnishings.

If you are lucky enough to be able to afford or to have been given an old mahogany table and complementary chairs, you are obviously off to a flying start and can turn your attention to stencilling walls and floor, curtains and blinds, lampshades and table ornaments. If not, one of the best ways to create a spectacular effect at minimum expense is to buy cheap, second-hand furniture that can be stripped, sanded, repainted and stencilled. This is certainly a time-consuming process — to bring a set of derelict chairs to a state in which they can be stencilled will take you at least twice as long as stencilling the border of a room — but if you are prepared to commit yourself to the task, the results will delight you and you will be able to use the furniture as a starting point for creating a room that is beautifully co-ordinated. Alternatively, if you have a round table, a stencilled floor-length tablecloth will add a touch of inexpensive style.

Furniture aside, one of the simplest ways of introducing stencils to a dining

Stencilled place mats co-ordinate with Adele Bishop's Shelburne wall stencils

room is on all those small but significant objects that are regularly ignored, but that can contribute so much to the ambiance of a meal. Place mats, table napkins, fruit bowls, candlesticks, wooden salt and pepper mills, tiny table lampshades, name cards — they are all candidates for stencilling, and they are ideal objects for the amateur to practise on. They will sing out against a simple wooden table or a plain table cloth and give your room a feeling of warmth and intimacy that could otherwise only be achieved with considerably more financial outlay. And because the result can be created so economically, it is possible for many people to design a number of special table sets for special occasions: holly, pine trees and fir cone motifs for Christmas time; toys, teddies or circus scenes for children's parties; ribbons and hearts for Valentine's day; sunshine designs for the dog days of summer.

TOP LEFT: *A border of white tassels, showing how effective a pale design can look against a dark background.*

TOP RIGHT: *Stencilling has given these upholstered chairs considerable style.*

RIGHT: *Stencil-Ease's® Oval of Buds creates a pretty dado, while Pineapple Frieze makes simple pine furniture into something much more special.*

AN ETRUSCAN DINING ROOM

This dining room was added as an extension to a nineteenth-century townhouse. The owners were determined to have a proper dining room as there was no room to entertain in their kitchen and they didn't want to use the drawing room for eating in. So they tacked this dining space onto the south wall of the drawing room, in a small gap between that wall and the outside wall of the kitchen.

The room is tiny and it raised all sorts of problems. The proportions were appalling — 6ft × 7ft (1.8 × 2.1 metres) — the existing walls were crooked, and because three-and-a-half of them were party walls with little space for windows the room would be difficult to light. It also would reduce the natural light that had previously been let into the drawing room through a pair of French windows which had opened onto a patio and which would now connect the drawing room and dining room. Glass was essential but, apart from one small area, there

Discreet stencilling details add the finishing touches to this London dining room. Small Greek Key borders the ceiling and the decorative plates beside the door are linked with English Bow, Cordelia Border and Cordelia Tassel.

were no outside walls where windows could be inserted. The best solution seemed to be to make a virtue of necessity by putting in a second pair of French windows here, and introducing an angled glass conservatory window which comprises just under half of the roof. The dimensions of the room were doubled by lining the far wall with a mirror, and the romantic effect of candlelight is increased by a selection of glass candle holders along the mantlepiece.

The walls of this room were painted dark Etruscan red using a water-based glaze. This glaze creates a rich, deep effect which again appears to expand the dimensions of the room. So far, so good. Although in reality tiny, this dining room could nevertheless now accommodate eight people at a round table and create the illusion that they were in a reasonably large space, amidst pools of candlelight caught and reflected in the glass and glaze in such a way as to blur, soften and extend the hard lines of the room's basic structure. The owners have a selection of stencilled candle shades, table mats and napkins and they can also change these around as they choose depending on the kind of atmosphere they wish to create.

Still, there seemed to be an element missing. Of course, my mind turned to

The mirrored wall behind the fireplace reflects the designs on the opposite wall.

stencils as a way of introducing black so as to heighten the effect of the rich Etruscan walls! I suggested hanging six plates on the walls opposite the mirror and linking them with English Bow stencils, Cordelia Border and Cordelia Tassel from our Architextures collection. The stencils were applied with Coal Black paint, mixed with a hint of Moonlight White to obtain a paler grey contrast colour on the rope tassel. I had to use spray adhesive very sparingly to hold the stencils against the wall as masking tape would have pulled away the glaze, and it

would have been virtually impossible to recreate the original glaze mix. The project was a small one, and I completed it in just under two hours. Used in this way, the stencils add an interesting accent to this dining room, and they are made doubly effective by being directly reflected in the mirrored wall opposite.

However, the main problem I experienced when designing this room was how to balance the odd ceiling proportions. A low, flat ceiling together with the sloping, glass roof somehow did not work. The small Greek Key stencil from

the Architextures collection came to my rescue. It was stencilled directly onto the ceiling, forming an internal border in Coal Black mixed with Vanilla to echo the grey border outline on the floor. The transformation, which took four hours to complete, is a miracle and suddenly all the different levels fall into place.

Detail of Small Greek Key – note the corner treatment – and English Bow and Cordelia Tassel.

A ROOM WITH TWO VIEWS

One of the problems that face many people living in big cities is the lack of space for a spare bedroom. In this elegant London apartment, the problem has been resolved by building two cupboards, one on either side of the fireplace, containing Murphy beds that can quickly and easily be let down to provide sleeping space without detracting from the appearance of the room.

However, the installation of these cupboards did present one difficulty. Because the cupboards have to contain beds, they are rather deep for the width of the room, which is a long, narrow rectangle. This difficulty has in fact been made into a virtue by creating a special feature out of the cupboards, which have been beautifully painted as *trompe l'oeil* cabinets displaying an imaginary collection of blue and white china. Nevertheless, the impact created by this stylish device needed to be balanced by an equally pleasing treatment on the opposite wall, one that would not protrude into the room and narrow it further.

The obvious solution was, we thought, to stencil the wall as a print room. The

By day: an elegant dining room with a print collection and stencils adorning one wall.

owners of the apartment wanted to hang a collection of prints and of blue and white china plates (the latter having inspired the *trompe l'oeil* design on the cupboards). The walls are covered with a yellow, rag-look paper from Zoffany and this colour sets off the china to the best advantage. The yellow-and-blue theme is also continued in the curtains which are yellow with blue fan edging. We retained this discipline of blue against a yellow background by using Slate Blue and Moleskin paints. The stencils used are Cordelia Swag, Cordelia Border and Cordelia Tassel, and a detail from Laurel Swag used as a motif and the centre only of the Corner Rose for final details. All of these designs are from our Architextures collection.

This stencil design provides the perfect counterbalance to the *trompe l'oeil* cupboards and it is worth noting the project as a fine example of how stencilling can be limited to one wall without looking out of keeping with the rest of the room.

By night: on the opposite wall, cupboards painted by Neil Mackay with a trompe l'oeil *collection of china open to let down a pair of Murphy beds, cleverly converting the dining room into a bedroom.*

Details of the print collection, with Laurel Swag, Cordelia Border, Cordelia Swag, Cordelia Tassel and English Bow.

AN OPEN-PLAN DINING AREA

The dining area in Jill and Adi Strieder's delightful cottage is part of an open-plan room which also incorporates the staircase. The stencilled border runs around the ceiling of the room and is repeated in a different colourway on the stair wall and first-floor landing, so linking these two parts of the cottage.

The stencils were not part of the original decorating concept of this room but were added some time after it had been repainted. The theme that runs throughout the room is the use of pastel colours: the walls have been ragged with a light, apricot glaze, the carpet is ivory and the ceiling has been painted with a simple off-white emulsion.

Beyond the dining table, one of the earliest Designers Guild linen union fabrics cloaks the door leading into the garden and keeps cold draughts at bay as well as providing a subtle and pleasing variety of colours.

The stencilled border in this room was added at the suggestion of my husband, Francis, who had noticed the technique of painting cornices on to ceilings in

Stencil Ease's® Windswept border runs around the edge of the ceiling in this pretty dining room, and so lends greater height to the walls.

France and Italy. The Strieders felt that the break between walls and ceiling was too pronounced, and they wanted to resolve this with a treatment that would also make the very low ceilings seem higher. This aim was very simply and effectively realized by positioning the stencil at the edge of the ceiling rather than at the top of the walls. The stencil used is the Windswept design by Stencil-Ease® and the colours are Terracotta and Sea Green, toned down with Vanilla to give a paler effect.

On the staircase and landing, the walls are glazed and varnished with the same apricot glaze as the dining area, but in this instance the stencilled border has been used on the wall rather than the white ceiling, so continuing the co-ordination while creating a completely different effect to that in the downstairs room. Adi could not resist introducing a last flourish of the stencil brush on the wall directly above the stairs, which displays three decorative prints. These have been drawn together in print-room fashion using Cordelia Border and Cordelia Tassel, and an English Bow.

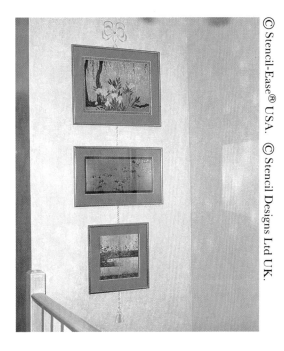

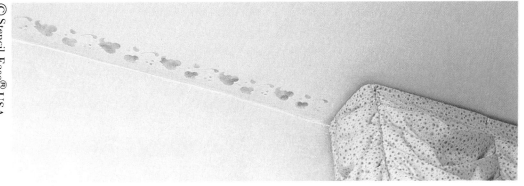

ABOVE LEFT: *On the walls of the stairs, Windswept is repeated, but this time below cornice level. A collection of oriental prints is linked by English Bow, Cordelia Border and Cordelia Tassel.*
LEFT: *The design breaks at the pelmet of the curtains, made from an early Designers Guild fabric.*

CHILDREN'S ROOMS

SAILING ships, farm animals, circuses, soldiers, forever favourite teddy bears — these are just a few of the many popular designs that have made it more fashionable to stencil children's rooms than any other part of the house. Lucky children! What better way of bringing a nursery or playroom to life than by introducing borders and friezes of these dancing stencilled characters? And for parents who despair of instilling any sense of tidiness in their offspring, what better way of coaxing older children to take care of their rooms than by involving them in the room's creation? If you are nervous about stencilling, start here. If you have doubts about how well you will be able to wield a paintbrush, you'll soon find the children themselves take over! You'll find, too, that the movement, character and sheer exuberance of many stencils make them perfect decorations for both boys and girls of all ages.

NURSERY RULES

Whatever the size of your nursery, you will want to ensure that it can stand up as well as possible to the wear and tear to which it is sure to be subjected during your children's early years of infancy and toddlerhood. Floors will inevitably be spilt on, walls drawn on and besmirched with sticky fingers, and everything within reach opened, examined and in all probability used for everything but the purpose for which it was intended. But forewarned is forearmed. When you plan your children's rooms, make sure your decorations are compatible with the activities of childhood.

FLOORS

In rooms for babies and young children, floor surfaces need to be quiet enough for you to be able to tiptoe in and out when the children are asleep without creating a disturbance. But floors also need to be easy to clean. A plain carpet will create warmth in the room whilst effectively soundproofing the floor; but it won't be long before it is stained. Cork or vinyl floor tiles are easy to keep clean, but they can create quite a cold atmosphere. A good solution to this dilemma is to use a canvas floorcloth which you can stencil as you wish. Floorcloths have three advantages in children's rooms: they are easy to clean; as your children grow out of 'baby' motifs, new cloths can replace old ones at minimum expense; and the exuberant patterns and colours of stencilled floorcloths will absorb and divert your youngsters for hours at a time. Up

Fly-by-night stencils on a midnight sky create a child's ceiling that is full of fantasy and enchantment.

to the age of about ten, children spend a great deal of time on the floor, whether they are learning to crawl, building brick towers, creating Lego villages or using your stencil designs as racetracks for toy cars and trains. Stencilled floorcloths will provide them with more interest and more opportunity for adventure than plainer surfaces.

WALLS

In a child's world, walls are not for holding the house up. They are for finding support whilst learning to stand, for doodling on, bouncing balls against and a whole range of other activities. Thankfully, most of the wall surface is out of reach of small children, so it is the area below dado height that most needs to be protected against the ravages of these early years. If you want your design to last for a reasonable length of time, you may opt to save your stencils for the area above dado height and childproof the area below by applying washable vinyl paint or eggshell. On the other hand, stencils can easily be renewed or replaced as your children grow older, so don't let yourself feel too constricted by practical considerations.

FIRST NURSERIES

Whether you are expecting your first or your fifth baby, you will find it difficult to resist the temptation of creating a nursery in preparation for the new arrival. Young mothers need to spend a lot of the first few months of their baby's life in this room, so it is well worth the effort of making your surroundings as attractive as possible. Babies, too, need visual stimuli from an early age. They respond far better to bright, warm and interesting decorations than to rooms that are bare and characterless. Stencilling provides a way of creating an enchanting nursery atmosphere with little financial outlay. Many of our customers visit our shop or contact us for the first time when they are planning a nursery. They find themselves with a wide number of designs to choose from, among them Stencil-Ease's® Carousel Horse, Baby Bear Border and Circus Clowns. Characters such as these can be used on their own or linked to any number of border designs that would be equally at home in other parts of the house. And miniatures such as Stencil-Ease's® Lace Border, Hearts and Flowers Border, Lollipop Flowers or Primrose Borders are

Small children love stencilled animals, which can be used to transform the furniture and walls of the plainest nursery.

ideal candidates for nursery furniture, cushions, cots and changing units. It is hard to resist the pale pink and blue pastels that are traditionally associated with early childhood, but if you choose a riot of primary colours these will give your offspring an added bonus as babies are supposed to be able to focus on red, yellow and blue before they can define any other colours.

Yellow walls and a brightly stencilled Baby Bear Border make this an extra-special nursery for baby- and toddlerhood.

UNDER-FIVES

The kind of decoration that you enjoyed in the first months of your child's life may well feel inappropriate by the time he or she has become an energetic toddler. And indeed you may have moved your child or children from a small nursery that was conveniently close to your bedroom to a larger room on another floor of the house. Again, if your home is spacious, you will perhaps be in a position to decorate a playroom as well as a bedroom.

Your toddler will now be a child of boundless curiosity, inquisitive about everything as he or she starts to understand the distinction between different objects and their functions, and to master the early rudiments of counting and reading. For youngsters of this age, stencils that invite the imagination to wander and explore through a variety of images make perfect playroom decorations. You can pursue a number of themes: Noah and the animals in his ark: a circus troupe; animals of the field and forest; a night-time ceiling of planets and stars. Other stencil essentials for this age group are the alphabet and number sets, which can be used as they are or adapted to spell out names, personalize pieces of

Nursery Bunny, bordered with tiny blue checks, in classic nursery shades of pink and blue.

Flying Kites add a decorative flourish to this wallspace.

The pale cream chest of drawers and walls in this little girl's room are given warmth and character by Cat and Tulip.

furniture or write nursery rhymes onto doors and walls. Number stencils can also be used to make measuring charts — great fun for parents and visitors as well as for recording your children's heights as the years race past.

BELOW: *Circus Clowns bring extra jollity to a child's painting desk.*

This is the age of school crazes, when your family life seems to be ruled by the overriding passion of the moment, be it cats, trains, Care Bears or My Little Pony. If you can manage to go along with your children's fetishes, you might be happy to stencil their bedroom walls with this ruling object of fantasy. Alternatively, you might be able ingeniously to

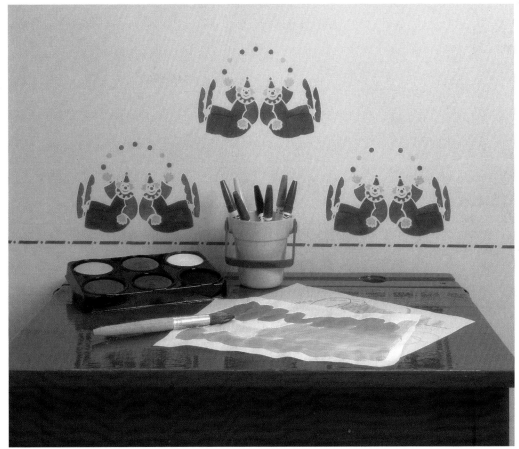

Older children love stencilling and can achieve very good results with a little adult guidance. Here, seven-year-old Alexander Nathanson stencils New England Bows around his little sister's bedroom.

divert them by introducing a stencil with a different theme and involving them in the decoration. Be careful, though, not to use stencils with children who are very young. Our stencil paints are non-toxic, but they should never be used by young children without supervision.

If your children share a playroom or bedroom and you can't opt for a theme one likes without upsetting the other, a simple and diplomatic stencil solution is to select one wall for each child and satisfy both of their whims without creating a room that looks totally unco-ordinated. Stencilled trains on one wall and ponies on the other need not be incongruous if the colours are complementary and each design is applied in such a way as to create a self-contained mural. Remember too that you do not need to smother the walls with stencils — you can also use them to create delightful *trompe l'oeil* pictures and blackboards on the doors and walls.

Mix-'n-Match stationery kits provide an ideal way of introducing youngsters to the art of stencilling.

CHILD INTO ADULT

Private territory matters desperately to many teenagers, and the freedom for individual expression also becomes increasingly important. Many teenagers want bedrooms which reflect their own identity, and which can double as rooms in which to study and to entertain their friends. By encouraging your teenagers to stencil their rooms, you will give them the opportunity to transform their surroundings into something they can be both happy to live with and proud to take care of. They will also be able to change, adapt or add to the designs as and when they wish with little extra effort to them or aggravation to you. Many of our most enthusiastic and imaginative customers have been in their teens.

Although many stencils have been conceived primarily for children, don't ignore their possibilities when you are decorating other parts of the house. A frieze of farm animals will bring a witty touch to your kitchen, and toy soldiers add a dash of gallantry to a bachelor's study!

This Primrose and Peonies design brings a breath of fresh air into a teenage girl's bedroom.

A CAROUSEL NURSERY

In this small child's nursery, Carousel Horses canter across the walls in an up-and-down border that is full of life and movement. On the lilac curtains, a jumble of Farm Animals and Alphabet Letters have been combined so that the letters spell out favourite animal noises, and the alphabet theme has been repeated again on the door.

This room was a typical 'boring box' before it was stencilled. It forms part of a late Victorian townhouse which has been completely converted inside to create a simple, modern atmosphere with white walls, matt ivory woodwork and stripped floorboards or berber carpet throughout. The owners resolved to keep the walls as they were and lend interest to the rooms through their choice of ornaments, pictures, wallhangings and curtain fabrics. Only the walls of the nursery and bathroom have received any kind of decorative treatment, and the stencilling here has been applied straight onto a white background to keep the room in harmony with the rest of the house.

The nursery does not have room for very much furniture and each piece — a

A merry-go-round of Stencil-Ease's® Carousel Horses rides around the walls of the bedroom.

three-door cupboard, a chest of drawers, a cot and a chair — is white so as to try and maintain the light, uncluttered character of the room. But a completely white environment would have been very clinical and unexciting for the inquisitive toddler who was destined to inhabit it. His mother was not able to stencil the furniture itself because it is all melamine and too shiny to take stencil paint well, so she decided to introduce colour with the cot quilt and bumpers, the curtains, and with stencils — not to mention the collection of soft toys that perch on top of the chest of drawers! Her choice of colours for the stencils was dictated by the pink, blue and green of the cot quilt and by her wish to create a room that would be just as suitable for a little girl as for a boy.

Rather than stencilling a straight border round the walls, she asked me to follow a flowing up-and-down sequence which not only conjures up the rising and falling of a real fairground carousel but also, with its sweeping curves, provides a welcome relief to the straight lines of the walls and furniture and the altogether rather dull, square character of the room. Each stretch of wall had to be carefully measured beforehand to ensure success, but as the room is quite small the project only took two afternoons to complete. On the second afternoon we got carried away and the door was also stencilled with letters and numbers as a gentle initiation to reading and counting.

The simple curtains have been made with lilac chintz from Laura Ashley, lined with pale pink cotton. It took another afternoon session to stencil the animals and sound effects onto them. The design has proved to be a great hit with the two-year-old for whom it was executed; the only drawback is that his bedtime ritual, which includes practising each of the animal noises as the curtains are drawn, now takes twice as long as it used to!

BELOW: *Detail of the Carousel Horse border.*
BELOW LEFT: *The panels of the bedroom door are attractively framed with stencilled alphabets and numbers.*
BOTTOM: *On the chintz curtains, the multicoloured farmyard animals provide hours of pleasure.*

STRAWBERRY FAIR

At the top of a large, eighteenth-century country house is this charming teenage girl's bedroom, which has recently been stencilled with a combination of Stencil-Ease's® Strawberry Border and Border Royale of tulips.

The room is small and rather narrow, measuring 12ft 5in × 8ft 7in (3.75 × 2.6 metres), with a small, west-facing window. The overall colour scheme for

LEFT AND ABOVE: *The charm of this young girl's attic bedroom lies in the skilful co-ordination of the colours of the furnishings with those of the stencils, and in the positioning of the stencil borders so that they become the main theme of the room without overpowering it.*

the woodwork and the walls is a light beige and the walls have been ragged to give them a slightly textured character. The sloping ceiling on the west side of the room is its most striking feature, and one that is highlighted by the pretty floral curtains in the window. It was the design and colour of the motifs on these curtains and the old-fashioned quilt on the bed that influenced the selection of the strawberry and tulip borders as stencils.

The tulip border runs right round the top of all the walls and also frames the doorway and the window opposite. These two walls are further defined by the two vertical stencil borders that run up the sides of each. For the two longer walls, the treatment has altered, with the chief feature of the south wall, which is the fireplace, acting as the basis for a symmetrical frame of strawberry vines. The discipline of this design is echoed in two further vertical strawberry borders on the opposite wall.

The reds and greens of the strawberry design complement the colours of the tulip border but at the same time the different scale of the strawberry stencil introduces a pleasing contrast to the room. Pretty without being fussy, these stencils add a most attractive, feminine touch to a simple bedroom decor; the whole project was completed over two days.

ABOVE: *Strawberry Border has been cleverly adapted to make a special feature around the fireplace.*

LEFT: *Detail of the two stencils, Border Royale and Strawberry Border.*

FIVE

BEDROOMS

BEDROOMS are, of course, for sleeping in. But in many homes now they fulfil other functions as well, sometimes doubling as a study or as a sitting room. And in small, open-plan apartments the bed is an integral part of the daytime living space. However, the conventional bedroom has many advantages: its occupant can beat a retreat to it when he or she wants peace and quiet and solitude; the door can be closed on untidy heaps of clothes; the bed can be stripped, aired or left unmade without one's having to worry about appearances; and for those who want to go overboard with their brushes and paints, the room as a whole can be decorated in a style that is suffused with romance and nostalgia.

TRADITIONAL BEDROOMS

The focal point of the traditional bedroom is the bed itself. As such, it should not be overpowered by the other furnishings in the room but should take pride of place and be a top priority when the room is decorated. If the room is to have an atmosphere of warmth and restfulness, the bed should stand on a rug or carpet of plain colours or subdued patterns — bright, riotous carpet patterns will distract and disrupt and make for an unharmonious mood. In a small bedroom, the floor space can be made to seem larger by using wall-to-wall carpeting of a plain colour in pale, neutral shades.

Beds come in all shapes and sizes and they can be dressed up or down depending on the effect you want to achieve. The easiest way to dress up a plain divan bed with stencils is to buy or make a cotton bedspread or duvet and stencil the design of your choice on it, using the same or a complementary design on the walls and the other furnishings in the room. Or you may like to buy a plain bedspread and use stencils on a heap of cushions for the bed. A fitted bedspread and a stencilled headboard will give you a more formal look, and if you want a really grand effect, a four-poster with stencil details on the woodwork or a sweeping canopy will give you a room fit for any potentate.

If you want a frilly, feminine bedroom, this is the ideal time to experiment with fabric stencilling. Curtains, blinds, dressing table covers and bedspreads can all be co-ordinated in the designs and colours of your choice. Make sure, though, that the fabric you choose does

In this pretty guest room, a custom-made paisley stencil acts as a frieze, and the walls are made to seem larger by being divided into panels with the Tulip Border from Adele Bishop's Small is Beautiful collection. More stencil details can be seen on the mirror, cushions and dressing table.

not contain synthetic fibres. For a more restrained effect, keep the furnishings plain and concentrate on stencilling the walls, either with a simple picture-rail border against a plain background, or with an overall design. Among the most popular bedroom stencils are the Strawberry Wreath & Vine, Garden Basket, Border Royale and Rose Peony Border.

Many modern homes have bedrooms with very little space. Once the bed is in place, there is hardly any room to add separate pieces of furniture such as chests of drawers, wardrobes and dressing tables. Because of this, many people now opt to have built-in furniture in their bedrooms, which provides instant floor-to-ceiling storage, takes up significantly less floor space than conventional furniture and makes the room far easier to clean. But walls of built-in cupboards can look all too streamlined and characterless. If you want to add softness and charm to a room with built-in furniture like this, use your stencils to decorate the cupboards with trailing border designs or with larger floral motifs such as Lupins, Violets or Blossoms & Bows. A quick touch of stencilling on plain woodwork can make a magical difference to any bedroom.

Prettily stencilled garlands give real charm to the mirror and chest of drawers in this delightful country bedroom.

Blue, green and purple used together in a stencil frieze that is full of movement. The colours echo those of the carpet and so draw the bedroom together into a decorative whole.

MULTI-PURPOSE BEDROOMS

If the bedroom you want to stencil has to perform more than one function, the bed will no longer be the focal point of the room. On the contrary, you will either need a sofabed, a foldaway bed or an inconspicuous divan. Beds that fold away into fitted cupboards are a good solution in this kind of bedroom and, as described above, the fitted units can easily be stencilled to make them an attractive feature of the room during the daytime when the bed is out of sight. But if you already have a divan bed that you want to retain in a bedsit or bedstudy, one of the best ways to incorporate it successfully in the room is by positioning it lengthways across a wall so that it doubles as a wide sofa and adding piles of stencilled cushions that can easily be tossed off when you are ready for bed. Alternatively, you can keep the bedcover and the walls a dark, plain colour to dado height, so that the bed is absorbed into the walls, and take the eye up and away from the bed itself by using stencil motifs on the area of the wall between the dado and picture rail. In this way, you will avoid having a room in which the bed sticks out like a sore thumb.

SPARE BEDROOMS

Spare bedrooms are of course the perfect places in which to go right over the top with your stencilling! A way-out design will delight and impress overnight visitors, and you yourself will not have to look at it every day, so that it will retain its novelty for you as well. Find out just how effectively stencils can replace wallpapers by using all-over designs on the walls and, if you wish, on the ceiling — stencilled wreaths can look particularly charming around a central overhanging light. Buy cheap and cheerful furniture, treat it to a lick of paint and select more stencils from Stencil-Ease's® miniature range — Traditional Elegance, Summer Delight, Butterflies & Berries, Country Hearts & Petals. By choosing miniatures that complement larger stencil designs, you will very easily achieve a total stencil look — overpowering if used in excess, but very effective in just one room of your home. And don't be deterred by thinking that the result will be too frilly and flouncy; very smart and more masculine rooms can equally well be designed with plainer stencils such as Josiah's Border, Little Bells, Willow Tree, Pinwheel and many more. Sweet dreams!

A motif of ribbons and flowers makes an unashamedly feminine focal point above the bedhead.

This strikingly pretty ribbon design picks up the dominant pattern of the curtain and chair fabric and makes a special feature of the slope between wall and ceiling.

This floral border relieves the starkness of plain white bedroom walls. Different elements of the design are used around the bookcase, candle and picture. The colours co-ordinate with the patchwork quilt.

OUR BEDROOM

This bedroom is my pride and joy. It is a simple loft conversion measuring approximately 8ft × 16ft (2.4 × 4.8 metres), with two south-facing dormer windows and fitted cupboards running the length of one wall. The proportions are not generous, the ceiling is quite low and the windows are small. These factors made it difficult to work out a way of decorating the room in a stylish way without the result seeming to be too incongruous for the size of the room.

However, both Francis and I have always loved Colefax and Fowler's 'Bowood' fabric and I longed to use this for the hangings around the bed and for the curtains. The floral pattern is quite a bold one for the size of the room, so I had to balance the effect by keeping the walls as subdued as possible, without leaving them so plain as to look unfinished by comparison with the rest of the room.

At the time, we were experimenting with different ways of using *trompe l'oeil* painted panels. In this instance, we wanted to give the room height and to introduce architectural detail that would lend style and distinction to the walls.

PREVIOUS PAGE: *Easy Peasy is used here to define* trompe l'oeil *panels and create an added illusion of space. The dark grey of the stencils also heightens the contrast between the sponged grey panels and dragged turquoise borders, showing off the paint finishes to their best advantage.*

ABOVE: *The colours of the wall paints used here echo those in Colefax and Fowler's 'Bowood' fabric. Note how the design is continued at the side of the window.*

LEFT: *The design is deliberately broken at the frames of the fitted cupboards.*

The colour scheme was dictated by the Colefax and Fowler fabric and so the panels were painted with a soft, sea green glaze overglazed in white, picking up one of the main colours in the fabric design. As well as giving height to the room, the panels also seemed to widen it, and to reinforce this effect we used the Easy Peasy stencil from our Architextures collection as a discreet border around each panel. I hadn't tried using stencils in this way before and I was thrilled with the result. The colours were Flannel Grey and Moleskin and we adapted the Easy Peasy theme to give an unusual but consistently architectural treatment to the space above the cupboard doors.

Some weeks after we had completed the wall stencilling project, I mustered the energy to paint my old pine dressing table a pale, green-grey and stencil this too. Here, I have used Flannel Grey and Autumn Brown for the urns, and a mixture of Sea Green/Aquamarine/Herb-Garden Green for the borders and the stencils themselves.

For me, this is the most relaxing room in our house, and the place I retreat to when I simply want to enjoy some peace and quiet on my own.

LEFT: *The central panel of the wall facing the bedhead.*
RIGHT: *The cheap wooden dressing table, painted and prettily stencilled with Rose Peony Border and Rose Peony Urn in colours co-ordinating with the walls and Bowood fabric.*

A Print Room to Sleep In

Marika Brennan has decorated the guest room in her late-Georgian home as a terracotta print room. Sparsely furnished and with a neutral, mouse-grey carpet, the room could easily carry an ambitious wall treatment to relieve what would otherwise be quite bare and stark surroundings. The introduction of stencilling here creates a formal yet friendly atmosphere which is striking in its simplicity.

The walls have been painted with a pale terracotta glaze, then lightly sponged. The Architextures Double Maypole forms a *trompe l'oeil* dado rail with panels below. To the left of the door, a selection of ten Chilean prints has been pasted straight onto the glazed wall surface and linked with English Bows, Cordelia Swags and Cordelia Tassels. This follows the traditional eighteenth-century fashion of pasting black-and-white engravings directly onto the wall surface. On the other walls, Cordelia Border has been used to surround antique prints that are already framed, so bringing them into unity with the treatment of the Chilean prints. Finally, Castille has been stencilled as a border around the top of the walls.

The stencils here have been applied with Slate Blue and Coal Black paints,

Castille and Maypole Double, from the Architextures collection, bring elegance and proportion to the bedroom.

although the black in fact looks dark grey because it has been used very sparingly. This colour, together with the straight, slender lines of Cordelia Border, is a beautiful complement to the iron of the bed frame and of the antique cot. The base and sides of the old cot also make an excellent surface for Marika to display her collection of antique lace and linenwork.

The same print room treatment is given to pictures on other walls to create a unified design.

The dark blues and blacks of the stencils complement the wrought iron bedsteads and make a pleasing contrast to the sponged terracotta walls. On this wall, Chilean prints have been pasted directly onto the glaze, in eighteenth-century fashion, and linked with English Bow, Cordelia Swag and Cordelia Tassel.

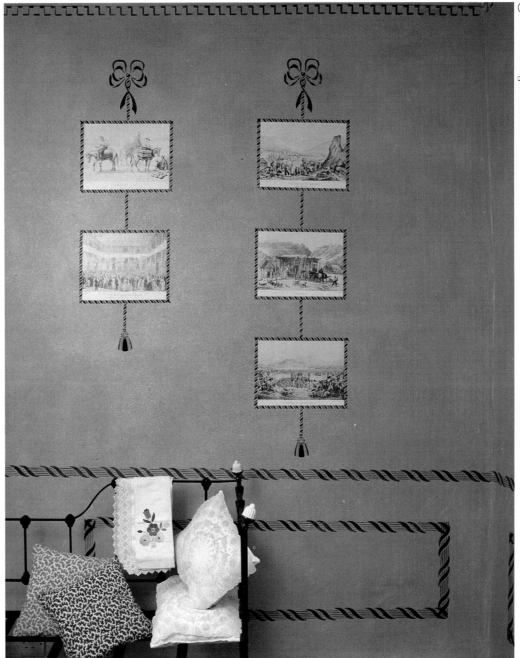

A Designer's Bedroom and Dressing Room

Decorative paint specialist Adi Strieder has added a lovely feminine touch to a bedroom and dressing room in his cottage by using a three-colour Stencil-Ease® stencil bouquet, Blossoms & Bows, on the fitted wardrobes and taking another Stencil-Ease® design, Border Assortment, around the border of the bedroom wall. A final touch has been added by using this border around the ceiling light.

In both rooms the colours of the stencils have been dictated by the delicate, peachy pastels of the curtains and hangings, which are made from an early Designers Guild fabric, Chinapot, and were chosen by Adi's wife, Jill. The walls are painted a light peach to co-ordinate with the fabric, and the carpets in both rooms are pale ivory.

The dressing room was originally a small bedroom which has been lined with wardrobes to provide extra hanging space. These are painted off-white and stencilled with bouquets in a combination of peach, grey and yellow. The

In the bedroom, Stencil-Ease's® Border Assortment takes up the colours of the Designers Guild fabrics.

butterflies, which are from a second stencil design, add a charming flyaway touch.

On the wardrobes, the upper panels show the full stencil bouquet, but this has been ingeniously adapted by Adi on the lower panels and for the border of the bedroom. Further variety is created by a subtle change in the shading of the bedroom stencils, which are lighter than those in the dressing room. These two rooms show how easy it is to extend and adapt an elaborate stencil so that it can perform several related decorative roles.

ABOVE: *Detail of Border Assortment.*

BELOW: *The same colours are repeated in the neighbouring dressing room, and another dimension introduced with Stencil-Ease's® Blossoms and Bows.*

The design has been cleverly adapted on the bedroom door.

A LEAFY RETREAT

The bold green and brown leaves and ferns that adorn the walls of Michael and Marika Brennan's bedroom show stencils in a most original and effective form. It is not hard to believe that the creator of this room is a lover of plants, and when the windows are thrown open onto the garden it is almost as though the natural world has entered the house and a clear boundary no longer exists between the two.

The room is very long and narrow, measuring approximately 8ft × 20ft (2.4 × 6 metres). As such, it badly needed a wall design that would distract the eye from these awkward proportions and seem to widen the floor space. Marika found her inspiration for this in the curtain material she had chosen. She started by painting all of the walls and the built-in wardrobe plain white, so as to have a simple, light and unobtrusive background surface for her design. She then adapted three fern patterns from the fabric and cut her stencils following the procedure described on page 146, using transparent plastic.

This bold collection of leaf and fern motifs is inspired by the leaves on the bedroom curtains.

The stencils are positioned in a seemingly random fashion at a reasonable distance from each other, in such a way as to emphasize the sense of space and airiness in the room. This feeling is further enhanced by the fact that the ceiling and walls above the picture rail have also been left plain. The wardrobe, however, has been integrated into the overall design. The stencilling theme is continued on the lovely collection of cushions that are arranged on the bed. On the walls the stencils alone complete the decoration of this room and eliminate the need for prints and pictures.

ABOVE: *Detail of the design.*

RIGHT: *The motifs stop at picture rail height on the walls, but extend to the upper panels of the fitted cupboards.*

SIX

BATHROOMS AND CLOAKROOMS

SINCE the introduction of domestic plumbing at the start of the century, bathrooms have progressed in leaps and bounds from being cold, spartan places with a four-legged bath standing self-consciously in no particular position, washstands unadorned by the touch of fabric and lavatories with yards of naked piping leading to huge overhead cisterns. Nowadays, bathrooms — and baths in particular — are the object of intense designer attention. The message seems to be, if you want to relax, get wet! Walk-in showers, circular baths, swirling jacuzzis — you name it and, if you have the money, you can have it. Gone are the days of cold, slippery baths, linoleum floors, draughty rooms. Today's bathrooms speak of comfort at the least, luxury at the most, and bathing has asserted itself as an activity to be lingered over and enjoyed.

The dominant feature of the bathroom will of course be the fittings themselves, and their colour will set the theme for the rest of the room. White may seem to be boring, but it will give you most scope where additional decorations are concerned. Deep terracotta and ebony black are very stylish, but they will also show every speck of scum and dirt. So if you are creating a bathroom from scratch, you may be well advised to choose a simple, pale colour for the fittings and introduce a splash of style by investing in extra-special flooring or panels of marble.

However sophisticated your bathroom fittings may be, the room won't look complete unless you pay equal attention to their surroundings. Nor will you take pleasure in lingering over your bath unless the room as a whole is a pleasure to look at and to spend time in. Traditional wall treatments run into problems here: conventional wallpapers can peel off in the steamy atmosphere, and pictures and posters don't fare well in this environment either. A happy solution is to use tiles, but a bathroom that is tiled from top to toe can be a cold and uninviting place. Stencil tiles are a good solution to this dilemma. Adele Bishop's Creative Tile® collection includes Crossed Garland, Sunflowers, Granada, Delft Vase with Flowers, Rabbits at Play and Little Dutch Tulip. For an equally dramatic effect, her Classic Checks are highly versatile used as borders on their own or co-ordinating with Creative Tile® stencils.

A number of other stencils can be used most effectively to decorate the walls and

Sophisticated charm in a country bathroom, with a delightful composition of stencil themes on the walls and the stencil theme continued with borders below the rim of the four-legged bathtub.

In this family bathroom, the simple addition of Adele Bishop's Hunt Border on the wooden window pelmet is all that is required to introduce a carefree country atmosphere.

woodwork of a new bathroom, or give a quick facelift to an old one. Aquatic themes are highly appropriate and even in the darkest winter months designs such as Stencil-Ease's® Victorian Scallop, Ocean Memories, Shells & Borders will fill your head with thoughts of warmer climates and hot summer beaches! Or you may wish for a jungle atmosphere; houseplants thrive in the steamy heat of bathrooms and you can add to their impact by choosing fresh and leafy stencils like Olde Ipswich Ivy, Hampshire Fern, Country Vine or Birds of Love. And why not introduce a few water-loving creatures among the leaves and grasses? The popular Duck 'n' Cattail Border looks at home in most bathrooms.

OPPOSITE: *Stencil-Ease's® Country Vine adds a feminine touch to this cloakroom. Note the treatment of the floor tiles and use of individual motifs from the basic design.*

Adele Bishop's Strawberry Wreath & Vine, stencilled into horizontal tongue and groove wall panels, brings freshness and charm to this child's bathroom.

The awkward, sloping ceiling of this bathroom has been made into an attractive feature with a stencil border inspired by the ceramic tiles. The tree motifs on the panels were also inspired by the tiles.

Cloakrooms

Why bother to stencil a cloakroom? Even in large houses which have room for huge cloakrooms, the clutter of coats, hats and other outdoor paraphernalia takes up so much wall space that it seems self-defeating to go to the trouble of decorating surfaces that are already half hidden.

Yet it is attention to neglected rooms and corners such as these that gives the final, professional decorative finish to any home. Whether you have a minute cloakroom tucked under the stairs or a large country cloakroom with space for riding kit, fishing rods and gardening clothes as well as coats and hats, spare a little thought to ways in which you might transform the space into something that deserves to be recognized as a real room. You won't need to spend very much time and effort: stencil details added discreetly to doors and skirting boards, their effects caught and reflected in cleverly positioned mirrors, will go a long way towards redeeming even the tiniest and seemingly most insignificant spaces. These are the ideal places too for joke stencils: Puppy Love, which shows a hopeful puppy outside his kennel, could be stencilled on the wall beside the hook from which your dog lead hangs; use Alphabets for spelling out witty mottoes; Reindeer, Porcupine, Fox and Beaver stencils can be placed so as to chase each other round the walls and lead your thoughts out across the fields and forests of the countryside.

RIGHT: *Don't confine yourself to conventional borders when planning a stencil frieze. Here, a succession of mirror-image tree motifs makes an unusually attractive design.*

© Stencil-Ease® USA.

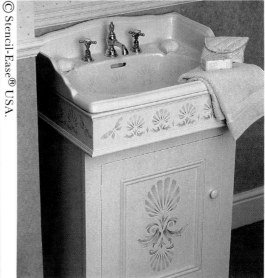

OPPOSITE: *You can easily and economically transform the walls of a plain bathroom by using stencils to simulate real tiles. The picture bows, floorcloth and bath have also been stencilled.*

ABOVE: *Elegantly shaded shells on this washbasin and cupboard make it as attractive as a hand-painted antique washstand.*

LEFT: *This second-hand commode was first ragged lightly, then stencilled with Duck 'n' Cattail Border.*

ENGLISH COUNTRY ROSE

This breathtakingly pretty bathroom shows custom stencilling at its very best. The brief was to breathe new life into the blue and pink Colefax and Fowler 'Bowood' fabric of the curtains, which had come with the owner from a previous house, and to design a stencil that could combine successfully with a large, strikingly contemporary 'film-star' mirror and double washbasin unit.

The stencils have been applied to a matt background paint that is pale cream with a hint of cinnamon to prevent it from looking too flat and white. The roses pick up those in the curtains, whilst the ribbons pick up the design of the blind, also made from a Colefax and Fowler fabric. There are just two rose stencils, one with a single flower, the other with three, but the design gains more vigour because the smaller stencil has sometimes been reversed as well as being applied directly. A third, trailing ribbon stencil runs around the borders of the mirror unit and so integrates this with the rest of the room.

Although they appear to have been positioned at random, these stencils have in fact been very carefully measured and positioned so as to create an effect which is bold and dramatic, without competing against the scale of the room. The use of

blue paint for the flower of the single roses and pink for those of the treble roses creates a sense of sophistication and prevents the design from looking too repetitive. One of the secrets of successful stencilling is knowing when to stop; here, the panelling around the bath has deliberately been left plain so as to control and contain the overall scheme.

The colours of these lovely peony stencils are taken from the Colefax and Fowler curtains, while the blue ribbon border is inspired by the blind, also made in a Colefax and Fowler fabric.

This very special example of stencilling took many hours of careful planning and execution and is not the kind of project that an amateur could tackle easily; but I think it shows how elaborately designed and well-cut custom stencils can impart real originality and elegance to their sur-roundings.

The ribbon motif has been further adapted on the borders of the make-up mirror.

ABOVE: *Detail of the design.*
RIGHT: *Both the colour scheme and the positioning of the two peony motifs are regularly reversed to introduce movement and variety.*

OUR BATHROOM

The bathroom of our home is on the top floor of the house, next door to our bedroom. It forms part of the same loft conversion as the bedroom and so shares the same problems, having awkward proportions, a low ceiling and an altogether rather cramped character (it measures approximately 8ft [2.4 metres] square). The best features of the room are the washbasin unit and mirror. It also benefits from plenty of natural light as the one dormer window is south-facing, looking out across our garden.

The starting point for the decoration of this room was the grey-and-white wall-paper which has a *trompe l'oeil* pattern and looks like draped cloth, so that the room feels rather like the interior of a luxurious tent. To increase the height of the walls and introduce some form of architectural discipline we added the dado rail and papered from the dado upwards. The mirror around the bath was installed to create a sense of light and space. The panelled door beside the bath conceals a cupboard which was previously a shower unit, but we removed that

Stargazing: lustre paints and bronzing powders from Stencil-Ease® were used to give an extra sparkle to these hand-cut star motifs.

because neither of us likes showers and also because we wanted as much storage space as possible. Finally, the woodwork, the walls below the dado and the doors were all glazed and marblized to co-ordinate the loo, basin and bath.

There followed an interlude of several months as we debated how to put the finishing touches to this room. The only colours here were the pinks and blues on the fabric that covered an old chair. For a while, we toyed with the idea of having a pink stencil on the glazed panelling to extend this colour in a diverting way. The old-fashioned floral design of the chair fabric is a favourite of mine, so I also thought of adapting this pattern.

However, after many meditative baths, inspiration was eventually found in the stars. I have not hung curtains or a blind in the bathroom window, so on clear nights I can lie in the bath and stare straight out at a starry sky. And as the bathroom is the room nearest the sky, stars seemed to Francis to be the perfect theme for a stencilling project that would look sophisticated and at the same time amusing. Pink stars did not appeal, so I found myself returning to the room's overall discipline of greys, highlighting this with silver and bronze from the Reflections stencil paint collection. We cut the star stencils ourselves, following the procedure described on page 146, and stencilled them on the doors, cupboards and bath panel, completing the project in

one afternoon. Now I lie in the bath and wonder about using old lace to disguise the dormer window, which is now rather too modern to harmonize with the rest of the room, but I haven't yet found the right lace and I prefer to live with rooms and let them evolve rather than rushing into sudden decisions. Although it took us many months to decide how to proceed, the stencilling in this room seems to me to give a very special final touch without having taken much time or effort to execute.

ABOVE: *A detail from the washstand.*
BELOW: *The star motif is continued on the panels below the window and on the bath panel.*

SEVEN

KITCHENS

PEOPLE dream about kitchens: immaculate white kitchens with spotless work surfaces and streamlined appliances and storage units; tiny, shoebox kitchens that nevertheless can be designed to contain fridge, dishwasher, cooker and cook with minimum clutter and maximum comfort; big, welcoming country kitchens, pans of stock or soup always a-bubble on an old-fashioned Aga while sleepy cats and dogs hug the warmth beneath; Dutch dressers crowded with a muddle of old and new mugs, cups, plates, jugs, and a wide old refectory table that is used variously for breakfasting, dining, studying, daydreaming. Apart from those rare mortals who always eat in restaurants, kitchens play a large part in all of our lives. Perhaps it is this, and our association of favourite childhood dishes with the scene of the strange process that produced these delights, that is the reason why we spin dreams around kitch-

ens. Family or no family, the kitchen is the centre of domestic life. Happy kitchens spell happy households. And for a kitchen to be a happy place, it must be a comfortable place — comfortable to work in, and comfortable to relax in.

So what makes a kitchen a comfortable kitchen? That depends to some extent on the size of your kitchen and on your taste. Small kitchens, be they the long, thin galley variety or the tiny cube variety, cannot be designed as anything but places in which to cook and, as such, the units they house need to be positioned so as to make it as easy as possible to do this. Larger kitchens frequently include a dining area and/or a seating area, and give more scope for creating contrasts in mood and atmosphere in different parts of the room. They too require units that are positioned for easy and efficient use, but whereas in small kitchens the type of unit chosen will set the theme for the

whole room, the more extensive floor and wall areas of larger kitchens allow for additional variety and invention.

KITCHEN UNITS

You can stencil on any kitchen unit provided that the surface is not shiny or glossy. If your units are coated in gloss paint, strip them down as directed in Part I and repaint them with a matt eggshell. Old wooden units that have been given a lick of new paint can be panelled with *trompe l'oeil* stencils or transformed with motifs. Higher-quality woods such as maple and mahogany can also be discreetly stencilled, preferably with natural shades that complement the

A crisp, inviting atmosphere has been created in this kitchen using the combination of yellow, blue and green against plain white walls.

colour of the original material — for example, Autumn Brown, Moleskin, Terracotta. In an age where countless home owners have opted for stripped pine fittings, the addition of sensitively placed stencils will lend a little extra distinction to your kitchen units.

FLOORS

It goes without saying that kitchen floors need to be easy to clean. Spilt soup, burst sugar bags, squashed peas, puddles of milk all need to be easily swept up or wiped away without leaving tell-tale stains. Rush matting and carpets are out. Quarry tiles and vinyl are in. So, too, are plain wooden floors. If your kitchen is as yet untiled, and if you want to retain the warmth of a simple wooden floor but treat it in such a way as to make your kitchen seem wider, lighter or simply livelier, plan a stencilled floor design. You will find a mass of inspiration by looking at classical paving designs, and you will give yourself hours of pleasure experimenting on paper with different colour schemes and combinations of shapes and ideas before you actually turn to measuring up your floor and applying the stencils. Formal parterre patterns, diagonally laid lozenges, triangles and diamonds — these are just a few of the shapes you can use as a starting point to create stunning *trompe l'oeil* flooring effects that will last for years.

No floor treatment looks more stunning than a well designed stencil pattern. Floor stencils such as these will last for years if they are properly varnished.

WALLS

Like floors, kitchen walls need to be practical and easy to look after. But this need not mean that they have to look boring. If your preference is for a chic, severe, streamlined kitchen, this sophistication can be subtly enhanced by using some of the simpler Architextures stencils such as Easy Peasy and Small Greek Key to add definition to your walls. Keep the result restrained by choosing a pale, pastel colour that gives a lift to the background surfaces without overpowering them. If you want to evoke the scents and colours of the countryside in your kitchen, experiment with lighter, brighter colours and larger, floral motifs — Windswept, Border Royale, Sunshine & Flowers Border, Strawberry Wreath & Vine are well-tested favourites with many of our customers. If you want an atmosphere that is formal but not too formal, decorative but not fussy, then a collection of botanical prints linked by stencilled bows, swags, borders and tassels will make for a highly stylish and discreetly colourful interior.

Whatever stencilling scheme you have in mind for your walls, don't forget the

A burst of sunshine is never more welcome than at breakfast time! It is no surprise that this Sunshine & Flowers Border is one of the most popular stencils.

importance of effective lighting, especially in a large kitchen which is also used for supper and dinner parties. It is a shame to create beautifully stencilled walls that disappear into the background when candles are lit on the dining table and any brighter lighting is turned off. Show off your work! It is well worth investing in a couple of uplighters that will throw your stencils into relief without detracting from an intimate evening ambiance and dazzling your guests.

THE CREATIVE TILE COLLECTION®

Have you ever hunted for kitchen tiles but failed to find quite what you want? Have you ever thought about tiling an area of your kitchen but been inhibited by the cost? If so, you may like to consider using one of Adele Bishop's creative tile designs to give the illusion of

tiles on your kitchen surfaces. You can choose from six designs — Crossed Garland, Sunflowers, Granada, Delft Vase with Flowers, Rabbits at Play and Little Dutch Tulip — all of which can be applied in whatever colours you want. Don't be constrained, either, by the overall design, but take details from it to extend the theme onto unexpected surfaces such as skirting boards, window frames, chairbacks, even storage jars. If

you have seen an old tile design that you would like to use, just take a tracing of it and follow the instructions in Part III for cutting your own stencils.

A modified version of Delft Vase with Flowers creates the illusion of real ceramic tiles on this kitchen wall. Granada is used on the spoon container. Both designs come from Adele Bishop's Creative Tile® collection.

FAR LEFT: *This beautiful, hand-painted Smallbone kitchen has been given a fresh, outdoor character by stencilling urns and flowers on the fitted units.*
TOP LEFT: *You can mix and match pre-cut stencils as you wish here, New England Bows are combined with Hearts & Flowers Border.*
LEFT: *A disciplined and symmetrical leaf border designed and painted for Francis Burne by David Mendel. Note how the colours of the stencil pick up those in the tiles and curtains.*

A MEDITERRANEAN KITCHEN

Although this kitchen is in fact in the heart of London, its rustic tiled floor, white walls, stencilled border and riot of plants all give it a deceptively Mediterranean character which makes you feel instantly relaxed and at home. Until recently, this space was part garden and part two tiny, narrow rooms, the further of which was the original kitchen. Michael Brennan conceived this new design, which involved having both rooms knocked into one long, narrow galley, then widening the living area by bringing down the outer, north wall and extending it across a narrow and rather gloomy garden passage. This extension has already been transformed by Michael's wife, Marika, into a beautiful conservatory, with winter jasmine tumbling across the walls on a wooden trellis, and a further dimension introduced by hand-painted *trompe l'oeil* arches which open onto palest blue skies.

The kitchen units were resurfaced with blue tiles because blue is Marika's favourite colour. This particular shade contrasts beautifully with the many

Winthrop Border is used in two colourways to pick up the blue of the tiles and the natural wood of the kitchen units.

pieces of antique pine, which include the kitchen table, old mangle and butter churn, all picked up in junk shops. Together, the mellow ochre of the pine and the blue of the tiles influenced the choice of colours for the stencil border. Painted onto a simple white background and appearing and disappearing behind a tangle of plants, shelves and generally delightful kitchen clutter, the border acts as an excellent foil for the greenery in the room as well as bringing out the warmth of the woodwork and relating to the blue tiling and (on rare sunny days!) the sky above the glass roof of the conservatory area. Blue comes into its own once more on the old milk churn that stands by the French windows and has been stencilled with a strawberry basket — minus the strawberries!

The stencil used for the walls is Stencil-Ease's® Winthrop Border and the colours are Sunshine mixed with Autumn Brown and Nankin Blue. Marika completed the project in an energetic burst of enthusiasm which lasted from 7 p.m. in the evening to 5 a.m. the following morning!

No room for stencils on this wall, but the trompe l'oeil *arches, framed by trellises of winter jasmine, have been neatly finished off with hand-painted jasmine fronds.*

The border runs in and around a delightful assortment of plants, photographs and general kitchen clutter.

The stencilled milk churn beside the garden door doubles as a plant pot.

The tiny village church of St Swithun in the Oxfordshire village of Compton Beauchamp was the source for this rich, Bacchanalian grapevine stencil. The church stands next door to the house in which Vanessa de Lisle, the owner and creator of the kitchen, spent her childhood. Its interior was beautifully stencilled during the high church revival in the latter half of the nineteenth century and it survives today as a strikingly original example of ecclesiastical decoration. The grapevine border at the church has been only very slightly adapted for its new incarnation. Transferred in this way, it carries lasting and much-valued memories of the countryside into Vanessa's crowded professional city life.

The south-facing French windows, which open onto a delightful garden, make this a perfect day room at all times of the year. During the winter months a rich, heavy *portière* hangs here to keep out cold draughts, but in summer sunshine streams in through light, lace curtains. It is a room for cooking, eating, writing, reading and generally pottering. At

The vine mural at the Church of St Swithun, Compton Beauchamp, which inspired the stencils in this kitchen.

A view of the dining area.

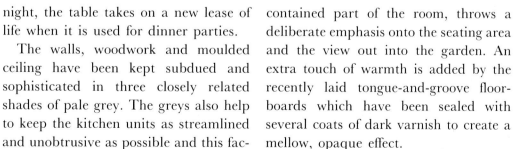
A view of the kitchen area.

Detail of the stencil.

night, the table takes on a new lease of life when it is used for dinner parties.

The walls, woodwork and moulded ceiling have been kept subdued and sophisticated in three closely related shades of pale grey. The greys also help to keep the kitchen units as streamlined and unobtrusive as possible and this factor, combined with the careful positioning of the kitchen fittings as a self-contained part of the room, throws a deliberate emphasis onto the seating area and the view out into the garden. An extra touch of warmth is added by the recently laid tongue-and-groove floorboards which have been sealed with several coats of dark varnish to create a mellow, opaque effect.

The stencil has been painted between the picture rail and ceiling in Heather mixed with Moleskin and Sea Green so that it approximates as closely as possible to a real grapevine. This motif has always been a favourite of Vanessa's and it could not be more at home than in this kitchen, where wine flows in the evening and, by day, room and garden seem to spill into one.

GARLAND TILES

BEFORE

ABOVE: *the newly fitted kitchen units needed some colour to make them look less clinical.*

AFTER

RIGHT: *Crossed Garland, from Adele Bishop's Creative Tile® collection, has transformed the wall surfaces around the white units. At the top of the walls, another colour is introduced with Grand Garland, from Stencil-Ease® USA.*

Garlands and festivals go hand in hand, and a distinctly festive mood has been introduced to this kitchen-cum-dining room with Adele Bishop's Crossed Garland tiles and Stencil-Ease's® Grand Garland Border.

The room is long and narrow — 18ft 8in × 9ft (5.6 × 2.7 metres)   and so falls naturally into two halves, the kitchen units being placed around three walls at the far end of the room, and the remaining space used as a dining area. When the current owner of the house, Sarah Brooks, moved in, the walls were in an appalling state and extensive restoration work was required. This ate into Sarah's budget and she initially intended to leave the area between the upper and lower kitchen units bare until such time as she could afford proper tiles. Instead of having to wait and save, however, she was able to control her costs by using stencilled tiles and so complete the decoration of this room earlier than she would otherwise have been able to.

The tile stencils have been painted onto a pale peach background wall colour using Terracotta, Slate Blue and Sea Green. After being left to dry for three days, they were coated with three layers of varnish to protect the design and make it easy to clean — any stains and splashes can simply be wiped off with warm, soapy water or a mild detergent. To unify the two parts of the room, the Grand Garland border has been stencilled

around the walls at picture-rail height using the same colours as the tiles. These two designs combine very effectively to create a complete decorative scheme which is full of charm and colour.

Grand Garland extends right around the room to the breakfast area.

PART III

DETAILS

ONE

MAKING AND CUTTING STENCILS

BEFORE this century, a wide variety of materials were used for making stencils. Among these were pasteboard, leather, metal and oilcloth, all of which provided sufficiently firm and stable surfaces for the application of paint without a high risk of smudging. However, the chief disadvantages of these materials are that, being opaque, they make it awkward for the stenciller to trace the design directly onto the surface and, when the stencil is ready for use, accurately to register the position of a second and third colour when working with multiple designs. Nowadays, the most versatile and durable medium for stencils is transparent plastic film, matt on one side for drawing and shiny on the other for cutting and stencilling. This and all other stencilling equipment can be purchased from my shop or from specialist art and craft stores.

CREATING YOUR DESIGN

Once you start thinking about designing your own stencils, you will find ideas almost everywhere you look. Antique tiles, china, wallpaper, fabric patterns and wrapping paper are just a few of the most obvious candidates that might inspire you. You may want to copy the design directly, and if it is printed on a flat surface to the scale you require, you will not need to redraw it before you trace the design onto your stencil film. But if you want to change the scale of the design, to add a few extra elements, or to create your own design from scratch, you must first redraw the design to the correct size on good quality tracing paper or adjust the scale on a photocopier. Before you start, have a look at a professionally made, pre-cut stencil so that you have a clear idea of how you should proceed.

When you draw your design, it is important to have strong 'bridges' of plastic between the different parts of the cut-out design. So if you are working on a very elaborate and delicate design with narrow bridges, it is best to cut two different 'part' designs on separate pieces of plastic.

This is also a good moment to experiment with different colourways. Take a few photocopies of your design and try

shading it with different colour combinations. This is a particularly valuable experiment if you are planning to make a stencil of two or more colours as you will find that different results are achieved depending upon which areas you shade in each of the colours. Make sure you know exactly what colourways you want for each part of the design before you trace and cut your stencil — you will greatly reduce the risk of making mistakes if you shade your drawing in the colours you want before you start to trace and cut the stencil itself.

ABOVE: *A stencil design adapted from an Italian plate.*
LEFT: *All stencils need to have strong 'bridges' between the cut-out parts of the design.*

TRACING YOUR DESIGN

1. Once you have drawn your design to the size you require, you need to secure it to a good drawing board or cutting board with masking tape. The surface you work on must be absolutely smooth to ensure a good result.

2. Lay the plastic matt side up over your drawing and cut it to a neat square or rectangular shape that allows a border of approximately 1in (2.5cm) from the furthest edge of the design. If you are designing a stencil border, the plastic should be half as long again as the design itself, so that you can include repeat marks on it and so be sure that, when you stencil, the border is accurately aligned.
3. Secure the plastic firmly with masking tape above the drawing or design.
4. Using a stencil drawing pen or a good technical drawing pen, trace the design exactly — working inwards from the areas furthest away from you.

SINGLE COLOUR DESIGNS

If you are cutting a single-colour design you need only draw onto one piece of plastic.

MULTIPLE-COLOUR DESIGNS

If you are cutting a multiple-colour design, you still need to trace the whole design onto your sheet of plastic, but in this case you should trace the areas to be cut for the first colour in unbroken lines, and the areas to be cut for the second and third colours in dots. The dotted lines will then act as register marks when you start to stencil. When you have completed your first tracing, take another sheet of plastic and repeat the tracing but this time mark the areas for the first colourway with dots and those for the second colourway with unbroken lines. For borders, repeat the design in dots on the extra length of plastic so that you will be able to position the stencil correctly. Repeat this process until you have a separate sheet of plastic for each colour that will make up part of the final stencil.

CUTTING YOUR DESIGN

For cutting your own stencils or uncut manufacturers' designs, it is well worth investing in a double-sided PVC cutting mat, available from our shop. These mats have a unique surface which miraculously 'heals' after use. A graph grid is printed on one side and you will find this very helpful if you design your own stencils. Another alternative is to use an old, wooden chopping board.

1. Lay the plastic, shiny side up, on the board and secure it firmly with masking tape.
2. Using a sharp utility knife or stencil knife, start cutting the design as smoothly as possible. You must have a sharp blade to do this successfully — never try to cut a stencil with a blunt knife. It doesn't matter what part of the stencil you cut first but you will best be able to control your work if you cut towards yourself all the time, turning the design where necessary so that you continue to work in the same direction. Always pierce the plastic before beginning to cut. Try to lift the knife as little as possible and make sure that you follow the exact line of your tracing. Don't let the knife waver inside or outside it.
3. When you have finished cutting, lift the plastic up to the light to check that you have no jagged contours. If you are unsatisfied with your work, start again. A poorly cut stencil will give poor results so don't give up until you are pleased with your work. You will probably make a few mistakes to begin with but you should soon be happy with your cutting skills.
4. If you are cutting more than one sheet of plastic for a multiple-colour design, double-check your work to ensure that you have not accidentally cut a part of the tracing for the wrong colourway.
5. Using a stencil drawing pen, add any additional register marks needed to each sheet of plastic so that each sheet can be accurately positioned on the surface to be stencilled.

CAUTIONARY NOTE

'Borrow' designs with discretion. Reproducing the work of contemporary licensed designs and some historic designers may infringe copyright.

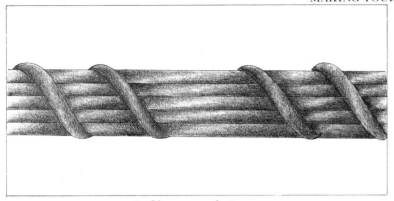

1. Choose your design.

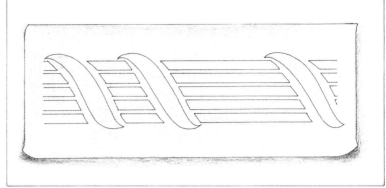

2. Draw the design onto tracing paper, separating it into two elements.

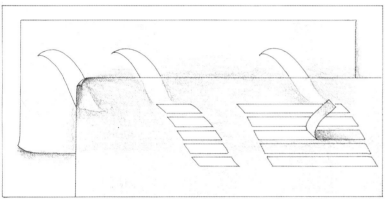

3. Cut the two elements out of separate sheets of plastic.

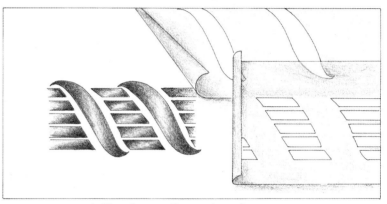

4. Test the stencil on a piece of paper.

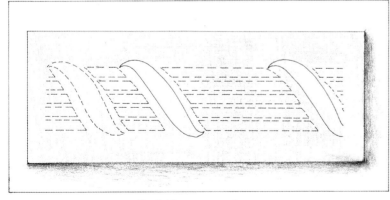

5. Add repeat marks.

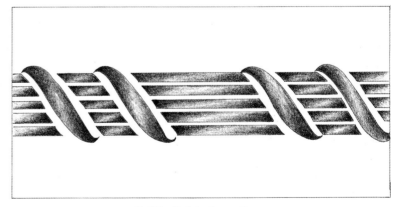

6. The finished stencil.

TWO

HOW TO DESIGN A PRINT ROOM

THE vogue for print rooms began in the eighteenth century and is generally believed to have originated in France. The new fashion swept through England and Ireland in the latter half of the century and many stately homes were graced with at least one print room. When the first Duke of Wellington was presented with Stratfield Saye, Berkshire, by a grateful nation, he is reputed to have decorated the house with no less than nine print rooms.

Originally, the prints used in print rooms were engravings. The subjects varied from collector to collector, but popular themes were drawings and prints collected as souvenirs on the Grand Tour, or images of a personal or professional character. In each instance, the prints were trimmed, pasted to the wall, 'framed' with printed borders and sometimes varnished. They were then linked by printed ribbons, ropes and bows. To-

day, a similar effect can be created by using stencils as a means of framing and linking prints.

The secret of a successful print room lies in establishing the correct balance between all the elements of the composition. The first element to consider is the wall, or walls, you wish to decorate. You can use any room in the house to hang a collection of prints, but if you have in mind a large display you may find you tire of it in a room you use a lot of the time. Halls, studies and dining rooms are ideal locations.

First, look at the wall carefully. Consider its height and width, and register any other features such as dado rail, fireplace and even electric sockets and lightswitches — they will all have a part to play in your design.

When you select your prints, remember that the more various their sizes, the more interesting your arrangement will

be. So bring together a mixture of shapes and sizes — large, small, square, rectangular, lozenge, oval and circular. If the prints are valuable, or if you want to take them with you when you leave, don't follow the eighteenth-century fashion of pasting them directly onto the wall but have them mounted and framed first. You can if you wish combine a number of different frame treatments but, as a general rule, you will achieve a more harmonious result if the mounts and frames for each of the prints are similar, if

A print room for the twentieth century: prints of all shapes and sizes are cleverly positioned and linked with Corner Rose, English Bow, Cordelia Border and Cordelia Tassel. The trompe l'oeil dado panels are stencilled with Maypole Single and Maypole Double. All the stencils are from the Architextures collection. Prints from the O'Shea Gallery.

not identical, to one another. Alternatively, quite inexpensive prints can be picked up in many antique shops and market stalls, and if you buy these you can spare yourself the expense of framing and paste them straight onto the wall.

Before you open your paste pot, however, experiment with the placing of the prints on the wall by drawing a small-scale diagram. Remember the following guidelines:

— Work from the centre out.

— Put the largest print in the central position.

— Arrange the prints in panels of uneven numbers. For some reason, even numbers always look less pleasing.

— For a balanced, classical effect, aim

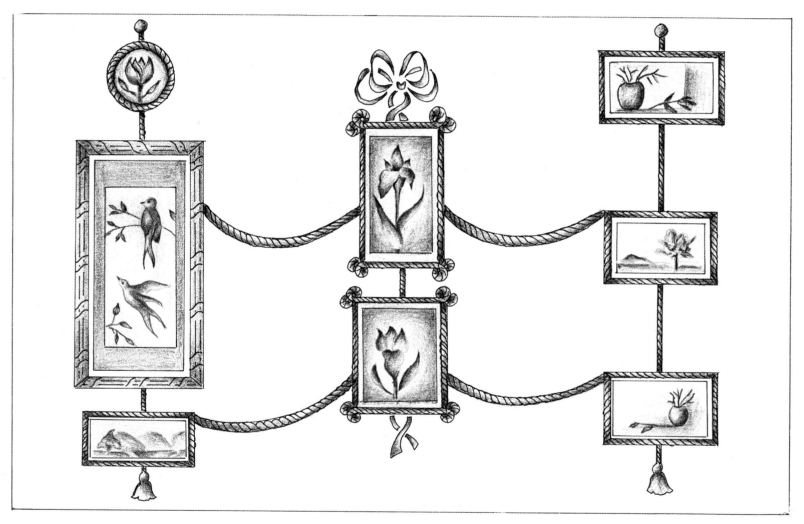

INCORRECT

to achieve as near a symmetrical result as possible.

To recreate a truly eighteenth-century character, use stencilled bows, borders, swags and tassels to link the prints to each other. If you have pasted your prints directly onto the wall, you can also use stencils to create *trompe l'oeil* mounts and frames.

Unless you are a purist, don't feel constrained to confine yourself to prints alone. You can adapt the print room theme to great effect with other decorations such as plates and mirrors. And many of the more delicate stencil borders can be adapted to link wall decorations in this way.

CORRECT

THREE

WINDOWS

STENCILLING is a very effective way of making a special feature out of a window. There are four main options to choose from: stencilling the blind, the curtains, the shutters, or framing the window with a border stencilled onto the wall. If you wish, you can of course combine two or more of these alternatives. If you are stencilling curtains or blinds, avoid synthetic materials and select a plain cotton fabric.

Before you decide how to proceed, give some thought to the kind of window you have. Does it have a pretty night-time view? If so, the best solution might be to do without curtains and stencil a border around the window. Do you spend more time in the room during the day or at night? For daytime use, a half-closed blind with a pretty stencil can look charming without blocking too much light; the design on stencilled curtains, on the other hand, can be lost during the day if the curtains are pulled well back, but look stunning when they are drawn in the evening. Old-fashioned shutters lend themselves to stencilling and remove the need to invest in curtains.

YOU WILL NEED

Stencil
Stencil paint (Fab-Tex paints for
    curtains and blinds)
Stencil brushes (fabric brushes for
    curtains and blinds)
Masking tape
Paper
Tape measure

BLINDS

1. Decide whether you want the blind to be fully or partly extended.
2. Choose a working surface on which you can roll out the blind and have extra elbow space. The best surfaces are large tables or the floor.
3. Experiment with trial designs on paper and work out exactly where you want to position the design before you stencil onto the blind itself.
4. Test a part of the design on a piece of fabric that is the same as the blind and apply the colours of your choice to this — remember that stencils look very different depending on the colour and texture of the background surface.
5. Use Fab-Tex stencil paints and fabric brushes and apply the paint slowly, working it well into the fibres of the material.
6. Leave the blind unrolled on the working surface until the paint is dry.

Use delicate shading to help your stencil designs transform plain roller blinds.

Variations on the New England Bows Border make this a charming window seat.

CURTAINS

1. If you are stencilling fabric that has not yet been made into curtains, decide what curtain pattern you are following to ensure that you buy the right quantity of material.

2. If you are stencilling ready-made curtains, ungather them so that they lie as flat as possible.

3. Choose a large table or the floor of a room as your work surface.

4. Measure out your design from the top of the curtain downwards. With unmade curtains, allow room for the upper seam.

5. Experiment with the colours of your choice on a spare piece of fabric — dark colours will alter the shade of the paints.

6. Follow the standard procedure for stencilling, using Stencil-Ease's® Fab-Tex paints and fabric brushes, and working the paint well into the fibres of the material.

7. Leave the curtains undisturbed until the paint is dry.

8. Heat-seal the curtains with an iron on a cool setting. If a large area has been stencilled, take the fabric to your local launderette and put it in a commercial dryer on high heat, for approximately forty-five minutes (home driers are not hot enough for large stencil designs). Check the manufacturer's instructions first to ensure that the fabric can be put in a drier.

FRAMING A WINDOW

1. Decide whether you want the stencil design to run right round the window or to extend across the top and part of the way down the sides.

2. Choose colours that co-ordinate with the rest of the room and use strong shades if you want to bring the window forward, pale ones if you require a more subdued effect.

3. Measure the area across the top of the window and plan your design carefully to ensure that it is balanced.

4. Decide on the best corner treatment for your stencil (see page 52 for instructions on piecing, butting, mitring and using a corner motif).

5. Apply your stencil following the standard instructions.

SHUTTERS

1. Make sure the shutters are in a suitable condition for stencilling — bare wood should be stained, sealed or painted as described in Part I.

2. Check that the shutter hooks or knobs are also in good condition and replace them if necessary.

3. Measure out the design before you start, working out and down from the centre point at the top of each shutter, or each section of the design if you are using a design which repeats.

4. Experiment with your chosen colours on a piece of paper and pin this to the shutters to ensure that your scale and measurements are accurate and that the colour scheme creates the effect you want.

5. Apply your stencil following the standard instructions.

6. Leave the shutters open until the design has had time to dry.

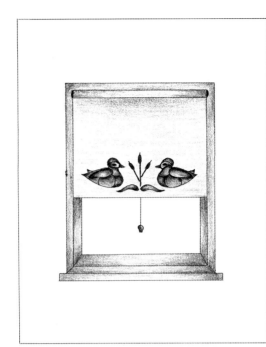

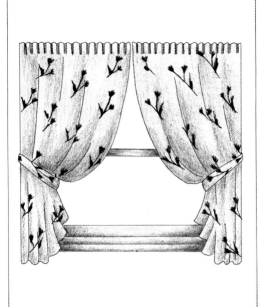

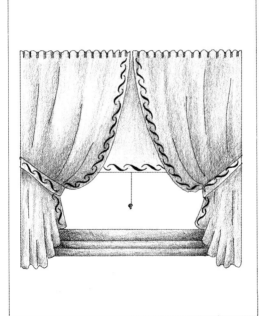

A SELECTION OF TREATMENTS FOR BLINDS, CURTAINS AND SHUTTERS

FOUR

CREATIVE TILES

THE Creative Tile® collection is a recent stencilling innovation that was developed by Adele Bishop in America. With this range of fantasy tiles you can create a decorative tiled effect on almost any surface in your home, quickly, easily and at little expense.

Creative Tiles look wonderful on fabrics and provide an imaginative way of co-ordinating curtains, table cloths and smaller items such as table napkins. You can either use these pre-cut stencils from Adele Bishop's collection, or cut your own to co-ordinate with existing tiles or to replicate a favourite tile design that you have seen on your travels. Tile stencils can be used to add charm and originality to large surfaces such as floors, tables, walls and cupboard units; they can also be applied to smaller objects all over your home. And details of the designs can be picked out to echo the theme of your choice on objects as varied as kitchen trays, linen chests and shower curtains.

> **YOU WILL NEED**
>
> Pre-cut stencil
> Stencil paints
> Stencil brushes
> Masking tape or spray adhesive
> Ruler
> Pencil
> Grey, studio felt-tip pen or [for fabrics] fabric pen
> Plastic film and stencil knife
> Paper

1. Using a ruler and pencil, divide the object you have chosen to stencil into a grid of squares that correspond to the size of the stencil tiles you are using.

2. Experiment on paper to decide where to position the tiles. You can create an overall effect, but more complex designs tend to look better if they are interspersed with plain tiles.

3. Check that the colour scheme you want matches the background colour onto which you are working. If you are stencilling onto a wooden or painted surface, consult Part I, Chapter 2, to ensure that the surface is suitably prepared before you start.

The Creative Tile® collection at work: Crossed Garland adorns the chair cover; Little Dutch Tulip decorates alternate squares on the walls; Sunflowers cover the chest; Delft Vase with Flowers transforms a canvas bag; Rabbits at Play are used on the place mats. Finally, four Granada tiles are framed to make an interesting wall decoration.

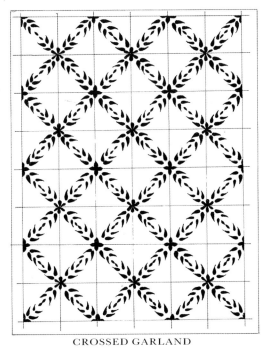

CROSSED GARLAND

DELFT VASE WITH FLOWERS

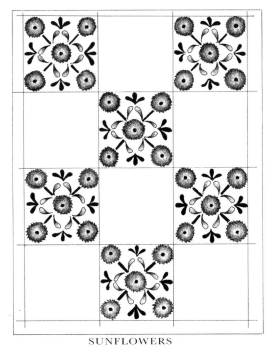

SUNFLOWERS

RABBITS AT PLAY

GRANADA

LITTLE DUTCH TULIP

—— 158 ——

4. Stencil from the top of the object, working out and down one colour-way at a time, and allowing the first colourway to dry before applying the second.

5. You can increase the authenticity of your tiles if you add grout lines. There are two ways of doing this:
   a) Draw on the grout lines following your pencil register marks with a grey, felt-tip studio pen. If you are working on fabric, use a fabric pen. For an effective *trompe l'oeil* finish, round the corners of each tile slightly.
   b) Cut a four-sided border stencil from transparent plastic, following the instructions given on page 146. Apply the stencil with a pale grey paint mix.

6. When the stencil pa... thoroughly, seal it with polyeurethane varnish if it area which is subject to moist... to wear and tear. If you use a felt-pen for grouting, spray the grou... lines with a protective aerosol to stop the lines from bleeding when you apply the varnish.

Ideas for Creative Tile® stencils

FIVE

FLOORS AND FLOORCLOTHS

FLOORS are easy to ignore. We tread on them, put furniture on them, subject them to years of wear and tear and forget about them. All too often, we smother them beneath neutral, monotone, wall-to-wall carpets as the simplest way of covering up expanses of floorboards and keeping out draughts. What a waste! A handsome floor can make an enormous contribution to the character of a room. Provided your floorboards are in good condition, stencilling a floor is far cheaper than carpeting it. And if your floorboards are unsound or the rooms of your home are already covered with protective but not particularly pretty carpets, you can bring them to life with stencilled floorcloths. Stencils can recreate an infinite variety of shapes and patterns on floor surfaces: rich, dark kelim designs; old tile patterns; floral motifs; trellis patterns; geometric cube and triangle

designs. These are just a few of many possibilities.

YOU WILL NEED

Tape measure
Long batten or length of string
   (for large projects)
Chalk
Stencil
Stencil brushes
Stencil paints
Sealer
Sealing brush
Sharp utility knife (for trimming
   floorcloths)
Glue (for turning under floorcloths)

FLOORS

If you decide to stencil a floor, you must first of all make sure that the surface is

properly prepared. To do this correctly, follow the instructions on surface preparation in Part I, Chapter 2. Before you start to stencil, decide whether you want to retain the look of the bare wood and simply seal the surface, or whether you would rather bleach, glaze or stain the wood. On the whole, you need to have floorboards that are in good condition to ensure a pleasing result with a transparent seal. If the floorboards are only in a moderately good state, you would be well advised to disguise the flaws with a dark paint or glaze. But be careful not to apply the glaze or paint of your choice too heavily unless you also want to conceal the grain of the wood.

The pretty pastels of this geometrical floor design contrast beautifully with the shadows cast by the sun on bright days.

Remember that a dark glaze will lend a feeling of depth and warmth to a room, and bear in mind too that a dark background surface is best for a floor which is subjected to lots of wear and tear — a well-sealed stencil floor will not easily be damaged, but pale colours show every speck of dirt and you will not thank yourself if you find you have to wash the floor every day to get rid of muddy shoe and paw marks.

The same stencil design as on page 163 adapted and used in more muted colourways for the floor of a study.

FLOORCLOTHS

Floorcloths can be stencilled either with our hard-surface paints or with Fab-Tex® paints. In either case, the most suitable material for the floorcloth itself is medium-to-heavy canvas, often referred to as 'duck' canvas. You can obtain this from awning and sailcloth stores. Grade 10 is a good weight for stencilling floorcloths. When you buy your canvas, check with the retailer to ascertain whether it has been pre-primed to protect it against shrinkage. If it hasn't, you will prime it yourself when you apply the base paint, but remember that the canvas will shrink a little as a result. In either case, you need to buy a canvas that is slightly larger than the finished design as you will need to turn back or trim the edges of the cloth to protect the fibres from fraying.

Like floors, floorcloths that receive a lot of wear and tear are best painted a dark colour. If they are not going to be regularly trampled on and you want a pale background colour, you will get a more satisfactory, 'finished' result if you first paint the canvas rather than stencilling directly onto it. Floorcloths are not suitable for glazing as the risk of cracking is very high.

RIGHT: *Floorcloths can be as attractive outside as in. Here, the crisp green colours pick up the freshness of the surrounding foliage.*

To paint a floorcloth, make sure that you have a flat surface to work on and do not disturb the canvas until each coat of paint is completely dry. Apply at least two coats of matt paint and take the paint right up to the edge of the floorcloth. If you plan to turn in the borders of the cloth, you don't need to paint on the reverse side of the canvas, but if you are working on a heavy canvas it is a good idea to trim the borders rather than turn them under. Don't do this until you have measured up the design, but once you have done so trim before you stencil and apply a final coat of paint to the trimmed edge as well as to the reverse side of the canvas. This will prevent the edges from having a raw, unfinished look.

MEASURING UP

Once the floor or floorcloth has been prepared, you must measure and mark the surface area carefully before you start to stencil. The only exception to this rule is when you are using a design on a random basis and, even then, approximate guidelines are a wise precaution. When you have started to stencil, you will be too close to your work to be able to judge distances accurately by eye, so begin by arming yourself with a tape measure and pencil.

For all designs, start by locating the centre of the floor. The most accurate way to do this is by measuring diagonally across the room from one corner to the

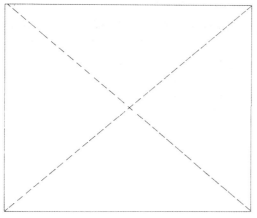

Centring a floor.

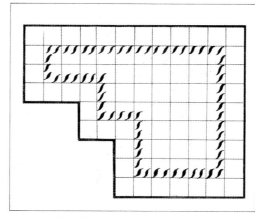

Dividing an irregular surface.

opposite one, with a long batten or a piece of chalk, or with a length of chalked string pulled taut and 'snapped' to leave a mark on the surface. Then repeat the process on the other diagonal. The point at which the two lines cross is the centre.

Irregular surfaces
If you are working in a room which is not a square or rectangle, such as an L-shaped room, divide the floor area into notional squares — two or more across the long side of the L and one across the short side.

Complex designs
If you are using a complex, geometrical design, divide the surface into separate sections for each repeat of the design and mark the centre of each section.

When you have established the centre or centres of the surface, you can use your stencil to measure out from the centre to

the borders of the design. Depending on the pattern you choose, you may wish to stencil right up to the edges of the room or floorcloth, or to contain the design in a border a few inches away from the edge. By working from the centre out, you will be able to ensure a balanced result and to resolve any inconsistencies in the design at the edges of the room, where they will be relatively inconspicuous. Mark your measurements in pencil or chalk so that you don't have trouble following them when you start to stencil. Don't be surprised if this measuring process takes a long time — in general, measuring floors and floorcloths takes longer than stencilling them and, of course, the more complex the design the more care you must take to make sure that it is accurately laid out.

With geometrical and symmetrical tile designs, you may have to juggle a bit at the edges of the floor so that you are not

left with half-complete designs at the borders of the room. The neatest way to avoid this is to introduce a stencilled border that 'contains' the design; a border that is slightly further from one wall than another will be far less conspicuous than a stencilled pattern that breaks abruptly at the edges of the floorspace.

STENCILLING

To stencil a floor or floorcloth, you should work with a large stencil brush except for small details. As with other surfaces, our fast-drying stencil paints are the easiest and cleanest to work with and significantly reduce the risk of smudges. For complex floor patterns, it is well worth double-checking your measurements before you start. Work from the centre outwards with each part of the design, applying the main colour first. If you are using a stencil design of two or more colours, allow plenty of time for each colour to dry before starting the next.

SEALING

Stencilled floors and floorcloths need to be well sealed to protect them from wear and tear. Even though our stencil paints are fast-drying, you need to wait at least four days before sealing your work, because the chemical interaction between polyeurethane sealers and stencil paints increases the possibility of the design bleeding unless the stencil paint has had time to dry out really thoroughly. To give maximum protection, a stencilled floor or floorcloth should be sealed with at least three coats of polyeurethane or another varnish. Allow at least a day for each coat to dry.

With floorcloths, you need to decide whether to turn under the edges of the cloth or to trim the borders with a sharp knife. If you choose the former option, turn in the edges and glue them down before you apply the sealer. When you seal the design take the sealer right up to the edges and, when the upper side of the canvas has dried, seal a few inches along the border of the reverse side.

Heavy canvases generally lie better if the edges are trimmed with a sharp knife rather than being turned in. This needs to be done when you are applying the final coat of base paint, as the paint colour should extend across the edges of the canvas and a few inches onto the reverse side. Similarly, when you seal the design, brush the sealer well into the edges of the canvas and onto the reverse side once the upper side has had time to dry.

AFTERCARE

Stencilled floorcloths should never be folded, otherwise the varnish will crack. They should be rolled for storage. Floors and floorcloths are easily cleaned with mild detergent and warm water.

A SELECTION OF DESIGNS FOR FLOORS OR FLOORCLOTHS

SIX

FURNITURE AND KNICK-KNACKS

ONE of the great pleasures of stencilling is the hunting down of old, neglected objects that can be transformed by a lick of paint and the touch of a stencil. Look about your home and you are bound to find something, large or small, that is crying out to be stencilled. Rummage in old attics and junk shops — once you know what to look for, all kinds of bargains will spring to light.

Old — and new — pieces of wooden furniture, tinware, mirror frames, screens, table mats and hairbrushes are just a few of the items that are perfect candidates for your stencil brush. When you have found them, take a good, hard look at their possibilities: the legs and sides of tables are worth stencilling just as much as their tops; cheap bookcase shelves will look treble their worth when stencilled; old biscuit tins can become objects you are proud to put out on display. Whichever you choose to stencil, proceed as follows:

```
┌─────────────────────────────┐
│      YOU WILL NEED          │
│  Stencils                   │
│  Stencil paints             │
│  Stencil brushes            │
│  Tape measure               │
│  Masking tape               │
│  Paper                      │
└─────────────────────────────┘
```

1. Before you start, make sure the piece you have chosen is suitable for stencilling by reading the advice on surface preparation in Part I, Chapter 2.
2. When the surface is ready, wipe it down with a damp cloth to remove any trace of dust and leave it to dry.
3. Choose your stencil design and experiment with different colourways on a piece of paper until you are satisfied with the scale, colour and position of your proposed design.
4. However large or small the piece you are stencilling, follow the standard method of measuring up from the centre outwards and working out and down from the centre focal point.
5. Allow time for each colourway to dry before you apply the next.
6. If the piece is to be subjected to wear and tear, protect the stencil design with a coat of clear varnish, following the manufacturer's instructions.

One of the best ways to start stencilling furniture is by experimenting on inexpensive pieces such as this child's chest of drawers.

ABOVE: *Plain wooden trays can be made to look as pretty or formal as you choose with a lick of paint and a little help from your stencil kit.*

LEFT: *A beautifully painted and stencilled wardrobe unit that echoes the motifs on the wall behind.*

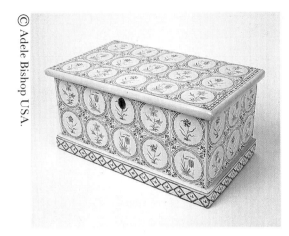

ABOVE: *This painted chest has been stencilled all over with a selection of wild flower 'tiles'.*

RIGHT: *Extend the motif you have stencilled onto a piece of furniture by repeating it on the walls.*

SEVEN

QUILTS AND CUSHIONS

SEEK out cheap, unpatterned quilts, duvet covers, pillow cases and cushions if you are looking for a way of bringing an individual decorative touch to a room without incurring too much expense. By stencilling these fabrics you will be able to co-ordinate them with the colours and patterns in the rest of the room, bring forward a colour that you want to emphasize, or simply introduce pattern and colour to an otherwise monotone setting. For the inexperienced stenciller, small projects such as cushions and pillow cases make ideal first projects.

It is important that the fabric you are using is suitable for stencil paints. Cottons and linens are ideal; silk and 50/50 per cent cotton/polyester mixes can also be used. Avoid heavy, textured fabrics, knitted fabrics, synthetic and water-repellent materials. These cannot satisfactorily take a stencil.

YOU WILL NEED

Stencil
Stencil paints
Stencil brushes
Masking tape *or* spray adhesive
    (for delicate fabrics)
Tape measure
Tailor's chalk
Paper

---

1. Pre-wash the fabric following the manufacturer's instructions and iron out any creases. Fabrics that are not washable should just be ironed.
2. Lie the fabric on a flat surface that also gives you plenty of elbow room.
3. Experiment with different colours, designs and positions on a piece of paper until you obtain a pleasing result.

4. Measure out the design carefully, marking the fabric lightly with tailor's chalk. Follow the standard measuring procedure, working from the central points outwards.
5. Secure the stencil with masking tape or spray adhesive, and apply the first colourway.
6. Allow time for the first colourway to dry before repeating with subsequent colours.
7. Leave overnight for the stencil to dry before heat-sealing it with an iron set to the temperature appropriate to the fabric being used. Do not use steam.

A lovely, summery collection of stencilled cushions.

ABOVE: *Classic Cat, Hearts and Classic
Checks adorn the pillow and duvet cover of this
child's bed.*

RIGHT: *Detail of stencils on 'crackled' fabric.*

LEFT: *Stencilled flower motifs make a most
effective design for this spotted quilt.*

APPENDIX

CAROLYN WARRENDER, STENCIL DESIGNS LTD

MANY of the stencils featured in this book are pre-cut designs stocked and distributed by my London-based company, Carolyn Warrender, Stencil Designs Ltd. The company also produces original stencil designs to commission and the shop offers a complete stencilling service, including the work of many of the stencil artists featured in this book.

Our London shop sells stencil ranges from the following companies:

Adele Bishop
Antonia Spowers Designs
Carolyn Warrender Stencil Designs
Felicity Binyon
Howard de Haviland
Mulhouse Design Company

Paintability
Pavilion
Payhembury
Spittle and Morris
Stencil-Ease

The shop also offers a comprehensive range of stencil paints, specialist brushes and other stencilling accessories. Visitors to the shop have the opportunity to try stencilling for themselves free of charge.

The address of the shop is:

CAROLYN WARRENDER
91 Lower Sloane Street
London SW1W 8DA
Telephone 01–730 0728/5011

Opening hours
Monday–Friday: 10.00a.m.–5.30p.m.
Saturday: 10.00a.m. – 1.00p.m.

ACKNOWLEDGEMENTS

WE should like to thank everyone who has contributed to the creation of this book and, in particular, all those who gave us permission to use their material or photograph their homes. Of course, the book itself would not have been possible without the dedication and loyalty of Carolyn's colleagues, to whom she owes an enormous debt of gratitude, and without the support of Adele Bishop and Stencil-Ease, who have done so much to contribute to the success of her company.

   Special thanks from both of us to: Karen Wilrycx for her inspiration and patience as an illustrator; Bet Ayer for skilfully translating our ideas into a finished design; Roy Farthing and his staff for their perseverance during many photography marathons; Adi Strieder and Tessa Hawkes for their stencilling; Caroline Knox and her colleagues at André Deutsch for their confidence in us and in this project. Above all, Carolyn would like to thank Alastair Gray, Dotti Irving and Jill Strieder for countless hours of support, encouragement and advice.

   Last but not least, a special thank you to our families and our husbands: to Francis, who has been a constant source of help and inspiration; and to Robert, who discovered babysitting skills he never knew he had!

PICTURE CREDITS

Adele Bishop 15, 84, 135, 157, 159, 163, 169 *above*, 172
The British Museum 13 *bottom left*
Colchester & Essex Museum 13 *far right*
Look Now 85 *below*
Pipe Dreams 36 *below*, 125 *above*
Smallbone kitchens 134 *left*
Stencil-Ease® 25 *left*, 39, 41, 61, 110 *right*, 123 *left*, 133, 154
Stencil – Decor 101, 131
Victoria & Albert Museum 13 *top left*, 14
All photographs by Roy Farthing except:
Marc Atkinson 71
Nic Barlow 97, 117 *right*, 132
Richard Bell 168 *left*
Pascal Chevalier 58 *near left*, 60, 173
Michael Dunne/Elizabeth Whiting Associates 57, 58 *top left*, 108 *above*
Andreas Einsiedel/Elizabeth Whiting Associates 51 *centre*, 58 *bottom left*
Clive Helm/Elizabeth Whiting & Associates 125 *right*
Andrew Kolesnikow 124
Di Lewis/Elizabeth Whiting Associates 109
James Merrell/*Homes & Gardens* 110 *above*
James Mortimer/*World of Interiors* 83, 121
Spike Powell/Elizabeth Whiting Associates 31, 108 *below*
Fritz von der Schulenberg 25
Christopher Smith 9

STENCIL CREDITS

Robert & Colleen Bery 51 *top right*, 161
Felicity Binyon 23 *below*, 36 *above*
Marika Brennan 37 *below*, 65/66, 73, 85 *top left*, 114/115, 118/119, 122 *left*, 125 *left*, 136/137
Jeremy Brooke 85 *top right*
Angie Clark 25, 63/64, 75/77, 149
Patzi Craven 51 *centre*
Alex Davidson 37 *above*, 74 *left*
Jan Davies 104/105
Ruth Davis 74 *right*
Susie Gradwell 110 *above*, 168 *left*
Tessa Hawkes 58 *bottom left*, 88, 123 (Colefax and Fowler), 124, 140/141
Howard de Havilland 71
Mary MacCarthy 72, 83 (for Victoria Waymouth Interiors)
David Mendel (for Francis Burne) 24, 67/69, 134 *below right*
Mulhouse Design Company 98, 99, 169
Joan Pallant 97
Pavilion 38, 85 *top left*, 95
Catherine Reurs 19, 145 *above*
Amelia St George 58 *right*, 60, 173 *right*
Stencil-Ease® Q53 – Endpapers, HV 19–8, 10, 174
Adi Strieder 23 *top*, 62 *below*, 78/79, 92/93, 96, 107, 116/117, 139, 167, 173 *left*
Verona Stencilling 62 *below left*
Carolyn Warrender/Francis Napier 31, 33, 63/64, 75/77, 80/81, 86, 88/91, 102/103, 107, 111/113, 124, 128/129
Victoria Waymouth Interiors 83, 121

FURNISHING CREDITS

Ann Chiswell 167
Colefax and Fowler 70, 75, 78, 111, 126, 132, 134
Hedgehog 96, 167, 173
Ian Mankin 111
Sinclair Melson 85
Osborne and Little 80
O'Shea Gallery 25 *right*, 124, 149
Pallu & Lake 86, 128
Paris Ceramics 123 *below*
Pembroke Squares 111, 118
Bernard Thorp 75, 80
Warner & Sons 104, 118

BIBLIOGRAPHY

Ayres, James, *British Folk Art* (Barrie & Jenkins, London, 1977)
   The Shell Book of the Home in Britain (Faber & Faber, London, 1981)

Bishop, Adele and Lord, Cile, *The Art of Decorative Stencilling* (Thames and Hudson,
   London, and Viking, USA, 1976)

Blake, Jill, *How To Solve Your Interior Design Problems* (Hamlyn, London, 1986)

Davidson, Alex, *Interior Affairs* (Ward Lock, London, 1986)

Fraser, Bridget (Ed.), *Stencilling — A Design and Source Book* (Elm Tree Books,
   Hamish Hamilton, London, 1987)

Green, Shirley, *Doing Up Your Home* (Good Housekeeping Family Library,
   Sphere Books, London, 1973)

Innes, Jocasta, *Decorators' Directory of Style* (W.H. Smith and Son, London, 1987)
   Paintability (Weidenfeld & Nicolson, London, 1986)
   Paint Magic (Frances Lincoln Publishers, London, 1981)

INDEX

Note **Page numbers in italic refer to illustrations.**